An excellent up-to-date introduction to democracy promotion is long overdue. This book's subtle, challenging yet forward-looking analysis offers much more. It should be read by anyone with an interest in the subject.

Peter Burnell, *University of Warwick, UK.*

Anyone who wishes to make sense of global politics in the twenty-first century will have to understand the meaning and dynamics of democracy promotion. Jeff Bridoux and Milja Kurki have provided a critical primer on this major new component of Western policy that will be of great interest to students, scholars and policymakers alike.

William I. Robinson, *University of California at Santa Barbara, USA.*

Asking hard questions and eschewing easy answers, this stimulating, insightful study takes the reader on an absorbing journey into the heart of the key debates and dilemmas defining democracy promotion today.

Thomas Carothers, *Carnegie Endowment for International Peace, USA.*

Democracy Promotion

This critical introduction to democracy promotion seeks to provide students with an understanding of some of the key dynamics and contentions revolving around this controversial policy agenda.

Specifically, this textbook examines democracy promotion through seeking to answer, from the perspective of an approach informed by 'critical theory', a set of important questions often posed to democracy promoters, such as:

- Who is involved in democracy promotion today and what kinds of power relations are embedded in it?
- Is democracy promotion driven by the values or interests of key actors?
- Is democracy promotion regime-change by another name?
- Is democracy promotion 'context-sensitive' or an imposition of Western powers?
- Is democracy promotion about achieving liberal economic reform in target states?
- Is democracy promotion a tool of the powerful, a form of hegemonic control of target populations?

The book suggests a set of provocative answers to these questions and also puts forward a set of challenges for democracy promoters and supporters to take on today.

Democracy Promotion serves as an effective introduction to an increasingly topical policy agenda for students and general readers and, at the same time, seeks to advance an important set of new critical perspectives for practitioners and policy-makers of democracy promotion to consider.

Jeff Bridoux is Lecturer at the Department of International Politics, Aberystwyth University.

Milja Kurki is Professor at the Department of International Politics, Aberystwyth University.

Interventions

Edited by:
Jenny Edkins, *Aberystwyth University*
Nick Vaughan-Williams, *University of Warwick*

> *As Michel Foucault has famously stated, 'knowledge is not made for under-standing; it is made for cutting'. In this spirit, the Edkins–Vaughan-Williams Interventions Series solicits cutting-edge, critical works that challenge mainstream understandings in international relations. It is the best place to contribute post-disciplinary works that think rather than merely recognize and affirm the world recycled in IR's traditional geopolitical imaginary.*

Michael J. Shapiro, University of Hawai'i at Mãnoa, USA

The series aims to advance understanding of the key areas in which scholars working within broad critical post-structural and post-colonial traditions have chosen to make their interventions, and to present innovative analyses of important topics.

Titles in the series engage with critical thinkers in philosophy, sociology, politics and other disciplines and provide situated historical, empirical and textual studies in international politics.

Democracy Promotion
A critical introduction

Jeff Bridoux and Milja Kurki

Routledge
Taylor & Francis Group

LONDON AND NEW YORK

First published 2014
by Routledge
2 Park Square, Milton Park, Abingdon, Oxon OX14 4RN

and by Routledge
711 Third Avenue, New York, NY 10017

Routledge is an imprint of the Taylor & Francis Group, an informa business

British Library Cataloguing in Publication Data
A catalogue record for this book is available from the British Library

Library of Congress Cataloging in Publication Data
Bridoux, Jeff.
Democracy promotion : a critical introduction / Jeff Bridoux, Milja Kurki.
pages cm. -- (Interventions)
Includes bibliographical references and index.
1. Democratization. 2. Democracy. 3. Political culture. I. Kurki, Milja. II. Title.
JC423.B7842 2014
327.1'1--dc23
2013029797

ISBN: 978-0-415-85779-6 (hbk)
ISBN: 978-0-415-85780-2 (pbk)
ISBN: 978-0-203-79651-1 (ebk)

Typeset in Times New Roman
by Fish Books Ltd.

MIX
Paper from
responsible sources
FSC
www.fsc.org   FSC® C013604

Contents

List of acronyms

ACILS	American Centre for International Labor Solidarity
CIPE	Center for International Private Enterprise
CPA	Coalition Provisional Authority
CSO	Civil Society Organization
DG	Direction Générale
DRL	Bureau for Democracy, Human Rights and Labor
EED	European Endowment for Democracy
ENoP	European Network of Political Foundations
ENP	European Neighbourhood Policy
EPD	European Partnership for Democracy
EU	European Union
EIDHR	European Instrument for Democracy and Human Rights
FDI	Foreign Direct Investment
FES	Friedrich Ebert Stiftung
FRIDE	Fundación para las Relaciones Internacionales y el Diálogo Exterior
GAO	Government Accountability Office, US Government
G-RAP	Ghana Research and Advocacy Program
International IDEA	International Institute for Democracy and Electoral Assistance
IFI	International Financial Institution
IMF	International Monetary Fund
INGO	International non-governmental organization
IRI	International Republican Institute
MCC	Millenium Challenge Corporation
NDI	National Democratic Institute
NED	National Endowment for Democracy
NGO	Non-governmental organization
NIMD	Netherlands Institute for Multi-party Democracy
OAS	Organization of American States
OECD	Organization for Economic Co-operation and Development
RAVI	Ghana Rights and Voice Initiative
SIDA	Swedish International Development Cooperation Agency
UN	United Nations
UNDEF	United Nations Democracy Fund
UNESCO	United Nations Educational, Scientific and Cultural Organization
USAID	United States Agency for International Development

Preface

This book seeks to provide an easily accessible introduction to the topical but controversial subject matter of democracy promotion. We have prepared it for the purpose of clearly communicating to the general public, students and practitioners of democracy promotion the relevance of a 'critical approach' to understanding democracy promotion and support. Our aim has been to avoid jargon and theoretically excessive discussion, while at the same time communicating the need to not only ask interesting questions about democracy promotion ideas and practices, but also to find interesting new answers and angles to the study and commentary on this subject.

We live in a challenging time for democracy promotion, support and assistance. While the Arab Spring, global financial crisis and changes in the world order power relations are presenting new challenges to democracy promotion, they are also producing new opportunities for rethinking and redirecting how democracy is promoted, encouraged and assisted in other countries and contexts. This book, while critical of specific democracy promotion dynamics, is not critical of 'democracy promotion' per se. Indeed, we are firmly of the view that black and white views – for or against – the practice of democracy promotion are problematic. Both the proponents and the critics of this complex policy agenda need to, we think, develop some more nuance and reflectivity in thinking through democracy promotion, its causes, functions and consequences. While the role of power is both inevitable and often hidden in democracy promotion (necessitating tools to study the various different modes and manifestations of power) this alone does not render democracy promotion an 'instrument' of the interests of Western 'core states'. Indeed, dynamics of democracy promotion seem to us such that they, while promoting the hegemony of particular ideas and thus interests, also are set up in such ways as to facilitate not only various reformulations of interests of power projectors but also various sites for possible resistance and challenge to hegemonic interests.

Revisiting, from our 'critical' angle, some of the crucial questions often raised for democracy promotion is then a productive and constructive, not necessarily a negative, critical effort. Indeed, it is the reformulation and 'revisioning' of democracy promotion that we seek to contribute to, through this text. We hope that this book will inform the reader – whether a student, a scholar or a practitioner of democracy promotion – but also provoke them to reflect more deeply on the complex conceptual and power political dynamics of democracy promotion and support today.

Acknowledgements

This book draws on the research and findings prepared as part of the 'Political Economies of Democratisation' project. This project, and thus much of the research presented in a general-reader-friendly format here, has received funding from the European Research Council under the European Community's Seventh Framework Programme 2007–2013 ERC grant number 202 596. All views remain those of the authors.

Many thanks to the project team – Chris Hobson, Heikki Patomaki, Anja Gebel and Marcel Van Der Stroom – for the support and dialogues on democracy promotion throughout the duration of this project.

Thanks are also due to the students on the module 'Democracy Promotion in World Politics' taught at Aberystwyth University in the autumn semester of 2012. They were exposed to some early draft chapters and ideas presented here, and the discussion with the students on this module assisted greatly in the formulation and articulation of many of the ideas presented here.

Special thanks are also due to our Research Assistants, Jessica Gerken and Oliver Newlan, for their excellent comments and provocations on the book manuscript.

Introduction

Why study democracy promotion today?

If the question 'should democracy be promoted or supported in countries where it does not exist?' does not interest you, it is likely that you live in a country where the political regime is already a democracy. It may be that you take democracy for granted and cannot conceive of being deprived of your fundamental rights or having the state deny you the freedom to express your opinion on the way your country is run. Or it may be that you take state sovereignty to be a self-evident good, not to be breached in defence of the democratic rights of citizens.

Even if democracy promotion is not of interest to you, you should probably bear in mind that the question of democracy promotion *is* of intense interest to many: such as those living in autocratic and democratizing countries who wish to develop democratic controls in their societies, and also those who think the existing democratic states can assist in developing democracy elsewhere. Indeed, arguably, in the context of the Arab Spring and the challenges democrats face, questions about how and why democracy should be promoted are more intense today than ever. Yet, the answers to such questions are elusive, often ambiguous and certainly contested, and as a result democracy promotion remains one of the most hotly-disputed areas of foreign policy making.

This book examines a number of the challenging questions which democracy promotion raises for commentators – whether sympathetic or critical. We will examine the relationship between values and interests in democracy promotion, that is, the motivations for this agenda. We will examine the relationship of democracy promotion with the even more controversial idea of regime change. We will also examine the role of cultural sensitivities in democracy promotion and the nature of power relations implicated in it. We do so through developing a broad analytical perspective we call the 'critical approach'. This is laid out in more detail in Chapter 1. Chapters 2 to 7 then interrogate through this broad perspective a number of challenging questions with regard to democracy promotion.

In this introduction we will provide the reader with a quick summary of the meaning and the historical context of democracy promotion and lay out some of the key reasons why democracy promotion needs to be carefully studied today.

What is democracy promotion?

The word 'democracy' comes from the Greek '*demokratia*', *demos* denoting people and *kratos* rule. Hence, democracy, by opposition to monarchy and aristocracy, means a form of government in which the people rule (Held 1996: 1). In a democracy, it is generally agreed, people benefit from fundamental civil rights and freedoms (freedom of speech, of worship, freedom from fear, and in some cases freedom from want) and at a minimum of the right to express their political opinion through voting in competitive, free and fair elections. It is interesting to note that, even though some in the West take these rights for granted, free countries in the world are in a minority: according to Freedom House think tank, 90 countries (representing 46 per cent of the world's 195 polities and 43 per cent of the global population) are considered 'free', while 118 countries are deemed 'electoral democracies', a somewhat less exacting notion (Freedom House 2013: 3).

Now, these figures might seem rather disappointing to some. A look at the trends over the last three decades reveals an even bleaker picture. Between 1980 and 2000, the world experienced a broad democratization movement with the number of free countries climbing from 31 to 45 per cent. The number of not free countries fell from 37 to 25 per cent. This positive trend continued into the 2000s, with a majority of countries experiencing an improvement in their political rights and civil liberties. However, since 2006, democratic progress has been stalling. Political rights and civil liberties are in decline rather than improving (Freedom House 2011). Democratization is not as straightforward as is sometimes assumed. And this is where, amongst other factors, democracy promotion is potentially of some significance.

But what is democracy promotion? And how can or should it be differentiated from concepts like democratization, democracy assistance and democracy support? It is important to start by dealing with some foundational definitional questions.

Democratization simply means that countries experience 'political changes moving in a democratic direction' (Potter 1997: 3). The end point of such changes is subject to contestation. Indeed, democracy, as a concept, is essentially contested (Gallie 1956). The contested nature of democracy means that there are various models of democracy on offer and in the light of recent events in the Middle East and North Africa, there is a growing consensus that this diversity will grow in the near future. However, from the perspective of Western democracy promoters, democracy is understood as the sum of two things: *electoral democracy*, with its focus on free and fair elections, and *liberal democracy*, which brings with it liberal constitutionalism and fundamental rights as key standards of meaningful democratization. In short, democracy is often equated with the idea of 'liberal democracy', an equation of considerable significance and a question which will be revisited in some detail throughout this book.

But even if we were able to agree that democracy can roughly be equated with the notion of liberal democracy, what does the promotion of democracy entail? It has been defined broadly as attempts to install or assist in the institution of democratic governance in states outside one's own (Hobson and Kurki 2012). There are many approaches to democracy promotion, however. Burnell identifies three approaches or categories of democracy promotion: use of force, conditionalities, and democracy assistance (2000: 283). Following the 2003 Iraq War, the use of force to promote democracy is today by and large discredited, although not entirely so as the intervention in Libya showed. Democracy promoters today prefer to use the two other means.

Democratic conditionality mechanisms are widely used today. For example, the US Millennium Challenge Corporation is an agency that ties democratic progress to economic aid. The selection of aid recipients is competitive and based on measures of the recipients' performance in relation to a number of 'good governance indicators'. The EU too uses democratic conditionalities: perhaps most famously through conditioning any future members of the Union to democratic rules and procedures specified in the so-called Copenhagen Criteria.[1]

Democracy assistance, on the other hand, is usually understood as the ensemble of technical, financial, material and symbolic instruments provided by democracy promotion agencies in authoritarian, semi-authoritarian countries and those under-going democratization. Democracy assistance, or what is also now often called democracy support, is thus concerned with support of indigenous processes of democratization (Lennon 2009: 99). The development of democracy assistance and support, and their increasing role in democracy promotion, illustrates a post-Iraq War trauma that affects Western democracy promotion. The backlash against destructive consequences of Western democracy promotion enacted through forcible militarily-imposed regime change caused Western countries to adopt a more careful, nuanced, country-specific, partnership-based approach to the promotion of democracy. In fact, the debate on the need to move to 'democracy support' illustrates that what is under fire is not democracy itself but the ways in which it is promoted.

Because there are now a variety of terms used to describe democracy promotion processes, some terminological notes are necessary. For us, democracy assistance and support, democratic conditionalities, and military intervention in defence of democracy are all forms of 'democracy promotion'. Democracy promotion then is the umbrella term under which a variety of forms of democracy facilitation fall under. Crucially, for us, 'democracy support', a term which many practitioners in the field prefer to the idea of democracy promotion, is not an inherently separate exercise from democracy promotion: this is because even the locally attuned workings of democracy supporters still consist in the 'promotion' of democracy in countries where they are active.

As we have seen democracy promotion is a broad and dynamic concept and practice. But let us seek to understand where it arose from: where did this idea of democracy promotion originate?

A brief history of democracy promotion

It is difficult not to consider the United States as the cradle of democracy promo-tion. US foreign policy has been principled in its support for democracy since the inception of the Republic. Born in a hostile world of authoritarian monarchies, the US Republic, as a matter of survival, had to make its political model an attractive one. Indeed, one can argue that democracy promotion constitutes one of the foundational elements of American foreign policy: Americans supported the promotion of democratic regimes as early as the eighteenth century and the French Revolution. They then sided with revolutionary forces that swept Europe and Latin America in the nineteenth century. Thomas Jefferson, amongst the first to formulate this position, saw the American Revolution as the opening act of a global struggle against tyranny destined to spread worldwide.

Jefferson's vision led to a rather assertive view of promotion of democracy in the global order. Not all American leaders were keen on such assertiveness, however. Jefferson's position was resisted, for example, by some of Jefferson's contemporaries, like John Quincy Adams:

> Wherever the standard of freedom and independence has been or shall be unfurled, there will her [United States'] heart, her benedictions, and her prayers be. But she goes not abroad in search of monsters to destroy. She is the well-wisher to the freedom and independence of all. She is the champion and vindicator only of her own ... She well knows that by once enlisting under other banners than her own, were they even the banners of foreign independence, she would involve herself beyond the power of extrication, in all the wars of interests and intrigue, of individual avarice, envy and ambition, which assume the colors and usurp the standard of freedom. The fundamental maxims of her policy would insensibly change from *liberty* to *force* ... She might become the dictatress of the world. She would no longer be the ruler of her own spirit. (Adams quoted in LaFeber 1965: 45)

Adams' position on democracy promotion explicitly challenges the forceful imposition of democracy in other countries and evokes ideas close to the notion of democracy assistance or support (see later chapters). In this case, democracy should not be actively exported but must be 'assisted' or 'supported' through material and moral means.

The two positions expressed by Jefferson and Adams prefigured the constant dilemma faced by democracy promoters: democracy promotion can become an instrument of state power projection.

A century after Adams' stark warning, President Woodrow Wilson sought to sidestep such a dilemma by putting democracy at the centre of a world order based on peace, free trade and collective security. His ideas, known under the label of Wilsonianism, are the foundations of the modern idea that democracy should be promoted.

Indeed, democracy promotion in its contemporary configuration is associated with the idea of Wilsonianism. In his 1917 speech justifying the US declaration of war on Germany, President Woodrow Wilson argued that it was necessary for the United States to fight German imperialism 'to make the world safe for democracy'. Wilson's new world was built on the belief that democracies do not fight each other; a community of democratic states will outlaw war for good. Free trade and the growth of international commerce modernize and civilize states, and lead them to interact peacefully to prosper. International law through international institutions also plays a modernizing and civilizing role, and is the basis on which to build a system of collective security. The League of Nations embodied this attempt to create a community of nations on which systemic peace can be built through collective disarmament, arms control, self-determination and freedom of the seas. These conditions – democracy, trade, law, collective security – were made possible because the world was progressing towards civilization. According to Wilson, the world, at the dawn of the twentieth century, was experimenting with a democratic revolution, in adherence to American 'democratic' principles. This endowed the US with special responsibilities to lead the world in a new age of democratic enlightenment. Wilson placed the US firmly in the driver's seat on a road to a peaceful democratic world; a world based on institutions and liberal values, what is known as a liberal internationalist vision of world order (Ikenberry, Knock, Slaughter and Smith 2009: 10–13).

Liberal internationalism, and thus the promotion of democracy, remained central to the foreign policy of successive American presidents over the course of the twentieth century. Franklin D. Roosevelt, Truman, Kennedy, Reagan and Clinton all championed freedom and democracy. The peak of this strategy is embodied in President Reagan's Westminster speech:

> No, democracy is not a fragile flower. Still it needs cultivating. If the rest of this century is to witness the gradual growth of freedom and democratic ideals, we must take actions to assist the campaign for democracy. ... We must be staunch in our conviction that freedom is not the sole prerogative of a lucky few, but the inalienable and universal right of all human beings. ... Let us now begin a major effort to secure the best – a crusade for freedom that will engage the faith and fortitude of the next generation. For the sake of peace and justice, let us move toward a world in which all people are at last free to determine their own destiny. (Reagan 2004: 116–17)

It is in the same speech that Reagan mentions the idea of a non-governmental bipartisan institution with the sole aim to promote democracy globally. The National Endowment for Democracy (NED) was subsequently created in 1982. NED embodies the then growing importance of democracy promotion in US foreign policy. Even Henry Kissinger, the epitome of liberal internationalism's traditional alternative, realism, had to concede that Wilsonianism dominates US foreign policy: 'It is above all to the drumbeat of Wilsonian idealism that American foreign policy has marched since his watershed presidency and continues to march to these days' (Kissinger 1994: 30).

However, in the 1980s, the power of expansionist democratic ideas was constrained by the realities of the international system. The Cold War was an ideological struggle which pitched democracy against authoritarianism, liberalism against communism, but it was also a permanent strategic game ruled by hardnosed security and economic interests: 'In the 1980s, democracy aid had to struggle to become something more than just a side element of anticommunist security policies, to become rooted in broader pro-democratic principles' (Carothers 2007a: 112).

Following the end of the Cold War, the 1990s witnessed a further embedding of democracy promotion in US foreign policy in a post-Cold War world without geostrategic competition and the positioning of the United States as global superpower. The budget dedicated to democracy promotion rose to new summits and its geographical reach expanded.

The number of donors also swelled. In addition to the already active German party foundations (created before NED), more European countries and, critically, the EU also dedicated more resources to democracy promotion, conditionality and assistance. Not only did the EU invest a great deal of effort and resources into the enlargement process, which could be seen as one of the most concerted democratization attempts since the Marshall Plan, but also it started to develop foreign policy instruments in relation to the developing world and its 'neighbourhood' states, and even launched in the early 2000s its new civil society funding instrument, the European Instrument for Democracy and Human Rights (for details see, for example, Youngs 2001; Youngs 2008). It follows that in the post-Cold War environment the EU has come to be seen as the central, and in many respects the most successful type of democracy promotion actor. Democracy is part of the fabric of EU external action but is not promoted through the same language or methods associated with US democracy promotion. The EU is perceived, rightly or wrongly, as a normative power in its democracy promotion (Bicchi 2006; Orbie 2009).

Democracy promotion seemed to be on the rise and in a position to carve a vital space for itself within Western foreign policy. However, the legitimacy of democracy promotion came under fire in the 2000s as the G.W. Bush administration embarked upon two local wars in the Middle East and a global war on terror in the aftermath of the 9/11 attacks on the United States. The association of democracy promotion with the wars on Afghanistan and Iraq, and the perception in the world of the war on terrorism as 'a forceful assertion of narrow U.S. security interests, not of any broader underlying principles, has badly hurt the legitimacy of democracy promotion' (Carothers 2007b: 114). It is now 'losing the force' (Whitehead 2009).

Democracy promotion embodies today the age-old dilemma: is it a foreign policy driven by values to foster a better world – the liberal internationalist project – or an agenda driven by the necessity to safeguard hard-nosed strategic economic and security interests? Democracy promotion, as practiced by state actors, has thus been caught in between a rock and a hard place – it is a complicated and challenging policy agenda to undertake.

Challenges of democracy promotion, and the critical approach

The difficult positioning of democracy promotion in foreign policy agendas of actors explains in part the contested nature of democracy promotion as a foreign policy agenda. Indeed, while it has been credited with some successes, notably in Eastern and Central Europe, it has also faced many challenges and criticisms, not least in the context of the 'backlash' which arose following the Iraq War (Carothers 2007b).

Numerous critical questions have been posed regarding democracy promotion, such as: Is it a 'Western' agenda reflecting 'Western' values? Is it a fundamentally 'compromised' agenda or an agenda with potential to emancipate populations? Is it an agenda that is more about the safe-guarding of the interests of Western actors than those of its recipients? Is it about values or interests, or both? Is the relationship between donors and recipients a relationship of power and, if so, what kind of power? What is democracy when it is promoted and what kinds of models of democracy can and should be promoted? Is how we define democracy a neutral matter? Are there hidden agendas attached to democracy promotion? Is democracy promotion about promotion of capitalism? Is it a form of ideological brainwashing?

These questions are, we think, extremely important to ask, and to answer, in today's context. This is partly because democracy promotion continues to be challenged by many critics – in the West and around the world – and it is important to appreciate the grounds on which it is challenged. Yet, it is also important to facilitate better, deeper understandings of democracy promotion, its potential and its power politics. Asking these questions is also important because democracy promotion reflects many difficult to perceive biases, contradictions and power relations. As we will observe in this book, democracy promotion is beset by deep running ideological beliefs about what the world ought to be. Although democracy promotion is often presented as a technical agenda, it is above all a highly ideological agenda. As such, it is an agenda that contributes to reconfiguration of power relations between donors and recipients who constantly renegotiate the political and economic future of countries that are assisted. For example, in the context of the Arab Spring it is crucial that democracy promoters can assist in ways which are helpful, while at the same time actors on the ground as well as in Western countries come to realize the limitations of, and constraints on, democracy promotion. Both challenges require deep and systematic thinking then on the kinds of critical questions that have been thrown in the direction of this policy agenda. Ignoring these questions is not an answer; but answering them in a nuanced way is also not an easy task, for 'simple answers' can distort and confuse more than clarify the complex power politics, causes and consequences of democracy promotion in today's context.

This book seeks to address the debates surrounding these questions but aims to do so from a new angle. We examine the provocative and important questions raised by commentators. Yet, we provide answers which seek to break down some of the more simplistic images of democracy promotion often presented in the literature and popular commentary. We seek to show that evaluating the role of democracy promotion and answering the challenging questions above requires adoption of a nuanced and open-minded empirical attitude: we need to carefully investigate the evidence for specific arguments – positive or negative – about democracy promotion. However, we also need to come to such an analysis with an appropriate set of tools: theoretical tools which allow us to look beyond the 'surface' appearances of democracy promotion, to the hidden logics and forms of power within it.

To provide more nuanced answers to these questions, we aim to introduce here a broad 'critical approach' to the analysis of democracy promotion. As examined in more detail in Chapter 1, this approach consist of broad 'interests' on the part of the examiner of democracy promotion: interest in 'critical' as well as 'instrumental' questions; interest in concepts and ideological underpinnings; and interest in various forms of hidden as well as observable power exertion.

As we will endeavour to show, from this broad critical theoretical angle we can observe interesting dynamics in democracy promotion. It is neither a straightforward tool of capital or 'hegemony', but nor is it a self-evidently emancipatory and power-free agenda. It is a practice infused with power – and increasingly hidden forms of power – yet it is also a practice with potential in opening up democratic futures at present denied to many in the world system.

Even so, specific challenges are presented today for democracy promotion, which democracy promoters should take seriously. In the context of the Arab Spring and the financial crisis, what is specifically challenged today are the conceptual models of democracy at the heart of democracy promotion, as well as the hidden forms of power which distort its practice. As we argue in the Conclusion, recognition of existing weaknesses is an important aspect of 'rethinking democracy promotion'. In the context of today's challenges, it is our belief that critical theorists, as much as practitioners and 'experts' of democracy promotion, can fruitfully contribute to this rethinking. With this in mind, it is our aim here to assist in developing dialogue and debate on alternative democratic futures in democracy promotion and the world order.

Specifically, we will endeavour to provide new kinds of answers to six important sets of questions that democracy promotion, and practitioners of democracy promotion, often face today, and to do so specifically on the basis of the broad critical approach we set out in Chapter 1. Then we tackle the seemingly simple but increasingly important question: who are democracy promoters? Chapter 2 examines the various actors involved in democracy promotion. We study the processes and instruments of democracy promotion actors but, critically, also argue that an analysis of activities of actors needs to be mindful of the relationships of power.

In Chapter 3 we seek to uncover how we should think of the relations between values and interests in democracy promotion? Is democracy promotion about promotion of Western interests or is it about projection of universal values, or a bit of both? We argue that most persuasive analyses today locate democracy promotion in the middle between values and interests, but also that a critical approach provides us with some of the more compelling accounts of how and why interests and values come together as they do, and indeed, may allow us to understand why both values and interests may be in decline as reference points of democracy promotion.

We then ask: is democracy promotion equivalent to regime change? We argue that, from a critical perspective, we have to come to recognize the way in which all forms of democratic interventionism – from military intervention to democracy support – entails a form of 'democratic interventionism' suggestive of regime change.

In Chapter 5 we ask the question: is democracy promotion reflective of context-ual sensitivities and differences? We argue that in the last ten years great attempts have been made to make democracy promotion more context-sensitive. However, these efforts, from a critical perspective, are shown to be somewhat limited and incomplete. For true context-sensitivity to be implemented, more willingness to open up the conceptual black-boxes of democracy promotion are necessary, as well as movement away from standardized delivery mechanisms which depoliticize democracy promotion and make dialogue on multiple meanings of democracy more difficult.

In Chapter 6 we focus on the question of economic interests: is democracy promotion about promotion of liberal economic reform? We argue that it is: although democracy promotion does not appear to be a functional instrument of capital, specific politico-economic visions do seem to emerge from it with important consequences for both donors and recipients of democracy promotion.

Finally, in Chapter 7 we seek to come to a view of what the role of democracy promotion today is in the global order: is it about the construction of hegemony of the powerful or about selfless emancipation of the weak and oppressed? Or a bit of both? We argue that democracy promotion is indeed a hegemonic practice, but that openings and resistances too can be found within it. Through a critical approach, we contend, we come to better perceive the power politics and exclusions of democracy promotion and thus to facilitate redirection of democracy promotion in a more egalitarian and dialogical set of directions.

Notes

1. This essential conceptual contestation is acknowledged by a number of observers. See Schmitter and Karl 1993: 39; Burnell 2000: 22; Held 1996: xi; Whitehead 2002: 14; Lawson 1993: 184; Dahl 2000: 37; Kurki 2010; Hobson and Kurki 2012.
2. The Copenhagen economic accession criteria approved by the European Council in 1993 require acceding countries to the European Union to be functioning market economies and to have the capacity to cope with competition and market forces within the EU.

1 Critical theory and democracy promotion

As indicated in the Introduction, various critical questions have come to be asked of democracy promotion in the course of the last 20 years. Is it about interest-driven molding of democratic opportunities, or is it a value-driven agenda aimed at pacification of world politics? Is it context-sensitive or an imperial practice? Is democracy promotion just another word for regime change? These kinds of questions have been raised more and more intensely in the last few years with the many failings and double-standards of Western democracy promotion having been exposed. In the context of the Arab Spring, for example, many have asked: how can it be that the US and EU were happy to support the regimes of Hosni Mubarak and Zine El Abidine Ben Ali while calling for an expansion of global democratic progress in other regions of the world? How do we understand such double-standards analytically? Moreover, since the late 1990s and the Asian crisis, and again since 2008 with the emergence of the global financial crisis, the failures of liberal democratization and those attached to liberal economic reforms have become manifest, raising further questions. How do democracy and economic liberalization work together? What kinds of politico-economic models emerge from democratization and liberalization agendas and with what effect?

We attempt to provide tools to enable the reader to answer these questions in a nuanced and productive manner, that is, in a manner that is *empirically attuned* to recent developments in world politics but at the same time *theoretically attuned* to the complexity and hidden nature of power relations in democracy promotion.

In this book we claim that fruitful responses to the questions set out above are achieved through exploration of a critical theoretical framework. To introduce this perspective, which is then elaborated on in each individual chapter, this first chapter seeks to introduce the broad analytical approach we call the 'critical approach' to democracy promotion analysis and to set it in the context of wider sets of perspectives that analyse democracy promotion. Here we seek to answer the questions: what does the 'critical approach' consist of, and how does it differ from other theoretical perspectives that have sought to analyse democracy promotion?

In this chapter, we will first examine critical theory and its core constituents, setting up a broad critical theoretical framework of analysis characterized by a four-fold set of concerns in analysing the social world: concern with knowledge, concern with concepts, concern with hidden forms of power, and concern with 'hegemony'. We then discuss the relationship between this framework and some existing non-critical and critical accounts.

A 'critical' approach: defining characteristics

It is not the aim of this book to rehearse the complex arguments in relation to positivist and post-positivist forms of theorizing, nor to discuss in detail critical and non-critical forms of theorizing. A student who wishes to engage these debates in more detail is referred to the rich range of texts that already exist (for example, Hollis and Smith 1990; Jackson 2011; Nicholson 1996; Smith, Booth and Zalewski 1996). Our aims here are modest and focused: we seek to simply provide a brief introduction into critical theory, followed by a discussion of its relevance to democracy promotion.

Critical theory is a theoretical tradition of thought in the social sciences which has at its heart the wish to challenge the 'reification' of oppressive social structures. Specifically, it seeks to do so through challenging *our own role* in reproduction of oppression in society: critical theorists point out that we are ourselves often complicit in accepting and reproducing patterns of thought and knowledge claims which have negative and oppressive effects on others, even as we think our claims are 'emancipatory' or 'politically neutral'. We are, and our knowledge claims are, intricately tied up with power relations and political patterns in society, even as we often think of ourselves as just 'free' and 'autonomous' individuals living our lives apart from others.

Concerned that in a modern industrial society individuals have become captured by oppressive thought patterns which reproduce inequality, critical theorists have been concerned to challenge how we come to 'know' society around us. Specifically, they have introduced a number of critiques of the ways in which we have become attracted to the festishization of 'scientific', 'objective' and 'instrumental' knowledge frameworks. Critical theorists are at pains to point out that all knowledge – even, and especially, 'scientific' knowledge – is political and ideological in nature in reproducing specific patterns of social relations.

This is why critical theorists have sought to challenge so-called 'positivist' approaches to social science. If most of social science has tried to emulate the natural sciences in that there has been a focus on trying to provide general, instrumentally useful and objective knowledge of the social world around us, the aim of critical theory has been to precisely challenge such a belief in objective science of society. Critical theory argues that all knowledge of the social world – of democracy promotion, or terrorism, or globalization for that matter – is in crucial ways 're-productive' and 'constitutive' of particular types of ideological and political (and politico-economic) assumptions and biases of knowers. This is because for critical theorists knowledge is always produced in the context of power relations, if often hidden and unnoted power relations, which structure what we come to think are 'reasonable' or 'practical' forms of knowledge and 'legitimate' and 'valid' knowledge claims. Critical theory specifically argues that the idea of 'neutral' knowledge needs to be challenged: no knowledge is neutral, it is always reflecting and producing assumptions presented for the knower by their social and political environment.

What this means for analysis of international politics is that there is no objective account of 'globalization' or 'terrorism' that can be had but that all accounts of what globalization or terrorism are and what their causes and consequences are, are in fact reproductive of particular ideological world views but thus also power relations. Thus, for example, an account of globalization as a form of 'interdependence' which brings peace, while seemingly neutral and objective, can be seen as an account which justifies and facilitates the furthering of neoliberal globalization through continuous expansion of free market economy, and thus tilts power relations between haves and have-nots within this world order in favour of those who 'have'. Similarly, accounts of terrorism identify some as freedom-fighters and others as terrorists, but do so, critical theorists suggest, always on the basis of ideologically biased criteria of what counts as the moral limit of justifiable forms of violence.

What this approach contributes to when analysing democracy promotion is the same wariness of 'neutral' and 'objective' accounts which provide justifications or instrumental guidance for democracy promotion as a practice. It provides an approach characterized by four analytical concerns, the centrality and meaning of which we need to appreciate.

Critical vs. problem-solving knowledge

The critical approach emphasizes the need to distinguish between instrumental forms of 'problem-solving' knowledge and 'critical' analysis of social life. Instrumental 'problem-solving' knowledge, argue critical theorists, takes as a given the social conditions and power relations of existing social reality and seeks, within this world order, to study how dynamics of interaction function and how knowledge of such interactions can be used to harness our ability to create solutions to social problems. Critical theorizing, on the other hand, subjects knowledge itself to critical scrutiny: it analyses not only the world 'out there', but also the knowledge-constitutive interests and assumptions which inform our knowledge of the world 'out there'.

In the case of democracy promotion, problem-solving knowledge would refer to knowledge which seeks to account for key dynamics in democracy promotion today, with the aim of identifying key problems and key answers as to how it can be conducted in a more efficient and functional manner. Instead of asking moral or ethical questions as to what democracy promotion stands for, or questions about 'power' or injustice in democracy promotion, the focus of a problem-solving theorist or empirical analyst of democracy promotion is to understand the nature of the practice and to make it better suited to achieving its aims.

A critical theory of democracy promotion, however, would be one which would aim not only to deliver instrumental knowledge of democracy promotion, but also to grasp how to understand the in-built dynamics of the very idea of democracy promotion, its ideological assumptions and the kinds of power relations and world orders that it facilitates. The focus of a critical approach to democracy promotion would be to try to understand how particular ideas and assumptions underpin the concept of democracy promotion and, crucially, what these assumptions do in producing power relations between actors in the world order. The aim here, then, is not only to understand the practical dynamics of, but the underlying conditions of possibility of, democracy promotion as a foreign policy practice.

This knowledge would point to the ways in which problem-solving accounts of democracy promotion and practice of this agenda can have embedded within it, often unknown to practitioners or scholars, very specific ideological assumptions and constitutive biases, which in turn come to reproduce particular types of social relations. Knowledge or practice of democracy promotion is not 'functional' and 'neutral' from this perspective but a form of power projection, if of a subtle type. Thus, for example, the constitutive role of 'liberal ideology' in democracy promotion has been pointed to by many critical theorists (Robinson 1996).

Concepts and ideology

As a related concern, critical theorists tend to have at the heart of their engagements an interest in 'conceptual' underpinnings of practices. These are important because within definitions and implicit conceptual assumptions made in research and practice, for critical theorists, specific kinds of ideologies and power relations emerge. Thus, the conceptions of democracy promoted by democracy promoters, for example, are seen as a central site of analysis, because the very understandings of this contested concept come to structure what kind of democracy is envisaged, allowed and seen as compatible with the values and interests of democracy supporters.

The conceptual politics of democracy promotion are seen as more than just a site of theoretical abstraction, but as the central site of determination of ideological and power relations. Democracy promotion analysis has to capture empirical processes, but also conceptual processes which underpin practical activities or choices of actors (Kurki 2010; Hobson and Kurki 2012; Kurki 2013). Indeed, as many critical theorists have emphasized, democracy promoters' view of the world is influenced by their ideological commitments to liberal democracy (Abrahamsen 2000; Ayers 2006; Kurki 2013; Robinson 1996). Such a commitment directly conditions the type of problems they identify – bad governance or autocracy – and channels the type of response democracy promotion provides – for example, many of their responses are structured by a strong belief that political and economic liberalism constitutes the 'obvious' pathway to political and economic modernization in developing countries. Because such conceptual and theoretical assumptions come to direct how democratization is undertaken and who counts as the right kinds of democratic actors, such assumptions entail that an ideological power dynamic often develops between donors and recipients of democracy promotion.

Power – both hidden and observable

A key aspect of a critical approach is that it is attuned to power, and crucially, not just to power, but different forms of power and their interaction. Specifically, the focus is on developing tools to think about the inter-relationships between hidden and observable forms of power. To understand what this means, it is useful to briefly explore the so-called 'faces of power' debate, and the Foucauldian response to this debate.

Steven Lukes (1974) famously differentiated between three faces of power. The first face of power implies, for him, an understanding of power based on the use of force. It can be summarized as a simple causal relationship: when A exercises his power over B, A acts with resources at his disposal to obtain something from B in order to prevail. Power is seen as exercise of raw force. Power is nothing else but a brutal causal relationship with the objective of prevailing in conflicts. Robert Dahl famously defined power as: 'A has power over B to the extent that he can get B to do something B would not otherwise do' (Dahl 1969: 79). Such a concept of power emphasizes the potentiality for conflicts of interests should B refuse to bow to A's requests. Power equates here with the ability to win conflicts.

But some analysts thought there was a problem with this analysis. Against such an approach to power that focused on observable material of power, Bachrach and Baratz argue that there is a second face of power. They argue that the study of power ought to include the potential limits to decision-making set by actors by leaving aside of the debate non-controversial matters, 'by influencing community values and political procedures and rituals notwithstanding that there are in the community serious but latent power conflicts' (Bachrach and Baratz 1969: 96). This approach looks at the environment in which a decision or relationship takes place, and includes in the analysis structural factors that influence one's power capabilities.

Lukes accepts the importance of 'agenda-shaping' in political decision-making, but argues that 'agenda-shaping' of a kind takes place in society at large. We come to view some values or interests as 'important' and 'legitimate', but why? Our decisions are influenced by what Lukes calls the third face of power. Lukes defines the so-called third face of power as follows: 'A exercises power over B when A affects B in a manner contrary to B's interests' (1974: 34). The exercise of power is here characterized not just by the integration in, or exclusion of, specific issues in the political agenda but also through the formation of individuals' views and outlooks in society at large (24). It is also characterized by the existence of latent conflicts of interest between those who are powerful and those who are not (24–5). These conflicts of interests are latent because victims of the exercise of power become unaware of their real interest. This unawareness is given rise to by the ability of the powerful to generate consent among the powerless. As Lukes puts it: 'Is it not the supreme exercise of power to get another or others to have the desires you want them to have – that is, to secure their compliance by controlling their thoughts and desires?' (23). This, in turn, allows for the taming of potential conflicts.

In the second edition of *Power: A Radical View*, Lukes refines his concept and distinguishes between two expressions of power: 'power to' and 'power over', the latter being a subspecies of the former. 'Power to' refers to a capacity, it is a potentiality in the hands of individual or collective social agents, who concentrate a defined sum of capabilities that they can use in order to achieve a specific set of objectives (Lukes, 2005: 6971). It is a quantitative view of power that insists on causality: because A can make use of a certain set of capacities, A can get B to behave in a manner congruent with A's interests. But as Lukes contends, such a concept is limiting as power is not only a capacity to act but is relational and asymmetrical: 'to have power is to have power *over* another or others' (73). Drawing upon Spinoza's conceptual differentiation between *potentia*, the power to exist and act, and *potestas*, to be in the power of another, Lukes defines 'power over' as 'the ability to have another or others *in your power*, by constraining their choices, thereby securing their compliance' (74).

On one hand, this compliance can be unwilling, in which case power is seen as coercive. Domination is 'the ability to constrain the choices of others, coercing them or securing their compliance, by impeding them from living as their own nature and judgment dictate' (85). On the other hand, compliance can be willing, in which case power is consent-based. If it is consent-based, one agrees that legitimacy is given to the power-wielders.

The Lukesian conception of power is important in moving us towards analysis of hidden forms of power, and analysis of exercises of power where 'consent' of the oppressed is present. However, there are forms of power that are even harder to identify. They work in a covert fashion and are embedded in institutions and techniques that constrain furtively the freedom of choice of individuals.

These covert modes of operation are identified in Michel Foucault's conception of power. He defines power as a 'structure of actions' that impedes the freedom of choice of individuals. His objects of analysis are thus the institutions, techniques and procedures used to influence the actions of individuals who have the freedom to choose. His focus is on the rationalities of government, 'that is, on discourses that address practical questions concerning how to conduct the conduct of the state and of the population which the state claims to rule' (Hindess 1996: 98). The emphasis is on the 'conduct of conduct', the way in which instruments and rationalities 'conduct' our supposedly free actions.

A critical approach to democracy promotion is distinct in that it would tend to draw on the latter faces of power: second, third, and the Foucauldian conceptualizations of power. Indeed, from a critical perspective, power emerges as a central concept, not because it is observable and quantifiable but precisely because its operations are often hidden and 'embedded' in social life. Identification of forms of power then takes more than simply observing one actor forcing another to do something: power also functions through generation of 'consent' and even 'unknown' to us through our thoughts and actions.

This is a central provocation for a critical analysis of democracy promotion for it leads us to look for forms of power which are hidden rather than openly expressed. As we put the concepts of coercion and consent at the core of our approach, we integrate both material and intangible elements of power. While the use of coercive power is pretty straightforward to analyse, the actions of an agent aiming at shaping subjects' values and interests in order to get them to consent to a set of policies is less evidently 'observable', and thus requires theoretical abstraction and analysis beyond mere 'observation'.

Hegemony

The critical approach's concern with concepts and power leads towards another theme central to a critical approach: an analysis of 'hegemony'. This concept derives from Gramsci's (1971) theory, although holds relevance for a wide range of critical approaches, from poststructuralists (Laclau and Mouffe 2001) to Marxist analysts, and more recently the English School (Clark 2011). To understand the relevance of this idea, examined in more detail in democracy promotion context in Chapter 7, we will briefly survey here Gramsci's key arguments as to the importance and relevance of the concept of hegemony for the study of social affairs.

As we suggested in the Introduction, and as is discussed in more detail in chapters to come, democracy promotion can be operationalized through various means: conditionalities, democracy assistance, or the use of force. The first and second means rely essentially on consent generation. The third method implies forceful regime change, as in Iraq in 2003, and the corollary use of force by those promoting democratic change. Gramsci's concept of hegemony, we argue in Chapter 7, is helpful in allowing us to understand the differential uses of power in democracy promotion today, and the extent to which a 'hegemony' is created through it.

But what is hegemony? Gramsci defines it in distinction to the concept of domination. Power can be exercised in the form of 'domination', material coercion of another. Yet, Gramsci argues that power is not *necessarily* exercised only through coercion, but also through consensual means, through construction of 'hegemony'. Hegemony is a power relationship in as much as it implies that one or more actors of the system aim and manage to get one or more actors of the system to behave in line with the interests of the hegemon, which might not be the case in absence of power displayed by the hegemon. Hegemony is thus understood as one side of the concept of power, the other side being domination, or use of force.

Coercion, Gramsci boldly argues, is in fact the less desirable option for many rulers and power-wielders, as it potentially undermines the hegemon's legitimacy and credibility. For Gramsci, then, it is the construction of hegemony that is central to the exercise of power in modern capitalist states. While focusing on importance of consent, it should be noted that for Gramsci, where there is hegemony coercion may not be eradicated, as coercion could be said to be always latent in social processes of hegemony. This means that in extreme cases the use of force remains a possibility, if consent does not bring antagonistic groups in line with the dominant class's position.

In Chapter 7 we will examine democracy promotion in relation to this concept of hegemony.

Critical theory and democracy promotion

Having outlined a critical approach and its focal interests and concepts, we now need to consider: why is it important to consider this approach in relation to democracy promotion? We argue here that it is important for two reasons: 1) because in democracy promotion analysis as it exists there is a lack of attention to exactly the sorts of dynamics that critical theoretical focal points indicate; and because 2) answering the questions set out in the Introduction will benefit specifically from this kind of approach and what it can bring. Let us talk through these points in turn.

There is an increasingly detailed and interesting literature today on democracy promotion. The motivations, and successes and failures, of democracy promotion are analysed today by various sets of commentators (see, for example, Burnell 2000; Cox Ikenberry and Inoguchi 2000; Mandelbaum 2007; McFaul 2010; Youngs 2001, 2003). There are two major theoretical approaches: the liberal and the realist schools.

Much of the analysis in the field draws heavily on the liberal school of thought in International Relations. They accept the liberal internationalist principles: that, expansion of democratic governance, increased trade and interdependence, and global institutional cooperation can and will facilitate global stability, prosperity and peace. It is these principles that states advance when they promote democracy (Mandelbaum 2007; McFaul 2010). Other commentators, however, point to the continuing role of national interest calculations in when and how democracy is promoted. They point to the fact that states only promote democracy when it is in their interests, and fail to do so when 'value commitments' of a liberal kind contravene interests (Youngs 2012).

This literature is helpful in clarifying the range of incentives which can inform democracy promotion, even as agreement on the motivations which drive specific cases of democracy promotion is elusive. The literature also does well in identifying problems of implementation of democracy promotion, and make a compelling argument for improved sets of practices in the policy-agenda.

However, this literature comes with a particular set of biases. Specifically, the analyses of motivations can be somewhat shallow. For example, interests are either not discussed at all, or are discussed solely in terms of national interests of donor states. In either case, it is assumed that 'motivations' of democracy promoters can be observed or traced in their actions or words. Also, there is a notable focus in the literature on improving the current practice of democracy promotion. Scholarship seeks to 'instrumentally' render better democracy promotion. As a result, relatively little is done to critically analyse the emancipatory consequences, or lack thereof, of democracy promotion as it is currently constituted. A small critical literature, discussed below, is present, but the majority of the analysis is not specifically interested in development of tools to take account of knowledge biases in democracy promotion and democratization, the role of conceptual assumptions in democracy promotion, and the role of hidden faces of power and consensual power relations. It is these sets of biases that the introduction of the critical approach seeks to balance out.

At the same time, the critical approach, with its distinctive concerns, also brings to the questions often asked of democracy promoters an interesting, theoretically and empirically nuanced, perspective. Thus, to ask whether democracy promotion is locally sensitive or equivalent to regime change, but to take account of ideological forms of control or the use of consensual forms of power exertion, matters for how we answer these types of questions. Indeed, as the chapters that follow will demonstrate, classical 'realist' or 'liberal' accounts fail to adequately understand the ways in which coercive forms of power morph into consensual methods of power exertion. And indeed the problem-solving accounts fail to understand how academic analyses themselves can contribute to the continuation of specific ideological biases and thus power hierarchies and hegemonies in international politics. A critical approach, as general as it is, can provide sets of provocations for us to keep in mind when dealing with the challenging questions democracy promoters face today.

Even so, as mentioned above, we are not the first analysts of democracy promotion to utilize a 'critical approach'. Many authors have made reference to the broad tools of critical theory, if in somewhat different formulations. What have these approaches discovered and what do we seek to add to their study of democracy promotion?

One of the key critical theorists of democracy promotion is William Robinson. His *Promoting Polyarchy* (1996) was the first to introduce to the analysis of democracy promotion all the four key dynamics of a critical approach: he was seeking to move away from problem-solving knowledge to deeper understanding of the role of democracy promotion; he was keen to analyse the conceptions of democracy which democracy promoters promoted; he analysed hidden as well as overt forms of power in US democracy promotion; and argued that democracy promotion should be interpreted in the context of the construction of US ideological and structural hegemony in the world order. Because of the centrality of Robinson's argument to a critical approach, it will be made reference to here at numerous junctures. Yet, as the reader will be able to tell, we also reject the full extent of the Robinsonian reading of democracy promotion as a tool of US hegemony. As we will argue, hegemony may not be understandable exactly in the terms Robinson suggests, and crucially the relationship between economic and political and the forms of power employed in democracy promotion may not directly correspond to the reading he puts forward.

Robinson's is not the only critical theoretical interrogation of democracy promotion. Others include those by Rita Abrahamsen (2000), Alison Ayers (2006) and Julie Hearn (2000). All these approaches, in one way or another, are interested in the conceptual and ideological underpinnings of democracy and the role of hidden forms of power in democracy promotion. Some of them, as does our account, stop short of maintaining that democracy promotion is an instrumental tool of US state power, but many point to hidden forms of power relations and, importantly, hidden ideological assumptions in democracy promotion practice.

It is these interventions and the small but important field of critical inquiry of democracy promotion that we seek to contribute to here. We hope to do so by introducing our broad but easily accessible analytical tools made reference to above. We argue that if a critical analyst is open to asking the four types of questions above – What would a critical approach to knowledge reveal? What are the conceptual foundations of democracy promotion? What forms of hidden powers can be identified? Is democracy promotion a hegemonic practice and if so how? – they will come to, if not the same reading as ours or Robinson's, an approach to democracy promotion which reveals aspects often ignored or by-passed in positivist and problem-solving frameworks.

We hope then that this somewhat unorthodox analytical approach to democracy promotion shows that, contrary to existing analysis of democracy promotion, our approach is 'critical' in the sense that the object of our investigation is not limited to a problem-solving approach, but rather focuses on the analysis of both hidden and observable processes that facilitate the dissemination of democracy. Crucially, we seek to reveal both 'hidden' methods and modes of democracy support as well as to critically interrogate the intended democracy aid practices. Also, we focus not merely on coercive measures (e.g. military intervention, sanctions) but, with a critical analytical tool-box in hand, analyse the power-relations embedded in more consensual methods (e.g. development aid, trade policy, civil society support). This is particularly important to appreciate today for much of the power of democracy support agenda lies, we argue, in the non-coercive consensual methods of demo-cracy support and hence expansion of the analytical framework away from a narrow problem-solving mentality allows us to better understand both the nature and the effects of Western democracy support today.

Conclusion

It has been traditional for the analysis of democracy promotion to be focused on analysis of the core motivations, actions, and successes and failures of specific actors in democracy promotion. Yet, most of the existing literature conceives of democracy promotion from the point of view of 'positivist theory of knowledge': the aim is to provide objective studies of the delivery of a defined object (democracy conceived as liberal democracy), identify the nature of the problem in international democratization and to suggest that shortcomings in this regard can be dealt with through more and better democracy support instruments (for a critique see Kurki 2010; 2013, Chapter 1). The study of the promotion of democracy turns into an observation of actions taken by democracy promoters, their outcome, and a summary of lessons learned. Study of democracy support is conceived in terms of 'problem-solving theory' (see Cox 1981) and conceptual awareness of the ideational framework worked with is lacking.

This book, instead, adopts a *critical approach* in developing an analytical framework to democracy promotion that insists on the need to move beyond problem-solving and observation-centred analysis of democracy promotion. Inspired by a critical theoretical turn, and critical theorists' interests in concepts, power and hegemony, this book develops an analytical framework that seeks to provide the general reader with a comprehensive, yet accessible, understanding of what democracy promoters do from a critical perspective which emphasizes the role of critical knowledge, conceptual foundations and hidden forms of power.

This analytical framework organizes the arguments and findings over the next six chapters and will try to provide answers to six interrelated questions about the subjects, nature, meaning and aims of democracy promotion in today's world.

As the reader will observe, it is our argument that complex relationships of power and hegemony are played out in democracy promotion today. It is neither a simple instrument of power of specific elites, nor is it purely emancipatory and 'neutral' in its interventions. In addition, democracy promotion today is not singular in nature: effects will depend on the actors involved, the instruments utilized, the geographical regions in question and interests at stake. Complexity-sensitive, but nevertheless critically equipped, tools are necessary today to understand democracy promotion's role, functions and modes and, crucially, the potential for redirecting this important foreign policy practice, a theme reflected on in the Conclusion.

2 Who does democracy promotion and how?

Democracy promotion rose to prominence in foreign and development policy in the aftermath of the end of the Cold War. It was already present in US thinking in the early twentieth century and from the 1960s played a role in the work of various European political foundations. Democracy promotion, depending in part on how you define it, has played a role in foreign policy activities of certain actors for a considerable time.

But who is active in democracy promotion today and what do democracy promoters do? This chapter provides a descriptive context for the analytical chapters that will follow, by introducing the actors involved in democracy promotion and examining the instruments and mechanisms they use to promote democracy.

This chapter demonstrates that democracy promotion today is an increasingly 'global' policy agenda. Intricate webs tie donors, deliverers and recipients of democracy aid to each other and embedded in these relationships, as we will go on to argue in the chapters that follow, are also relations of power. The following chapters will unpack these elements of power in more detail but even as we examine the actors and their activities in a descriptive sense here, we need to keep in the back of our minds the potential relations of power which emerge from the diversity of activity, mechanisms and networks characteristic of democracy promotion.

Global nature of democracy promotion

One of the common misunderstandings that general commentators have is that democracy support is something solely undertaken by the US; that democracy promotion is an 'American sport'. While the US has a strong historical role in having developed specific infrastructure for democracy promotion, and is known to have funded activities in this area generously compared to some other actors, it is crucial to appreciate that the US is by no means the only democracy promoter. Today, various sets of actors play their role in democracy promotion and support: international organizations such as the United Nations (UN), the European Union (EU) and the Organization for Economic Co-operation and Development (OECD); various Western states through their development aid projects, such as Germany, Sweden, Netherlands and the UK; intergovernmental organizations such as the

International Institute for Democracy and Electoral Assistance (International IDEA); autonomous but partially state-funded specialist organizations such as Netherlands Institute for Multi-party Democracy (NIMD) and the National Endowment for Democracy (NED); political foundations, such as the German Stiftungen and the Swedish foundations; NGOs and civil society organizations such as the European Partnership for Democracy or Amnesty International; and private companies such as Chemonics and DAC. Even international financial organizations, such as the International Monetary Fund (IMF) and World Bank, usually unconcerned with the state of politics in target countries, increasingly take an interest in encouraging the right kind of states and governance structures in third countries. They too are then active in encouragement of good governance.

Because of the range of democracy promoting organizations involved in the 'democracy support industry' today, it is important to develop an understanding of what these different types of organizations do and how they do what they do.

To gain a better sense of the activities of different actors and their role, we will discuss here in turn the core actors and the nature of their activities. For the sake of clarity, we divide the organizations into four groups as follows:

1 key 'state' actors in democracy promotion
2 international organizations as donors of democracy aid, such as the UN, EU and International Financial Institutions (IFIs)
3 semi-independent 'conductors' of aid and assistance, such as the NED, the International IDEA and political foundations
4 the 'on the ground' recipients and deliverers of aid and assistance, such as NGOs and private companies

These categories of actor are rather fluid in that some actors can fit into various categories at different times. Yet, they also give us a sense of the hierarchies and structures of relationships in democracy support. Indeed, importantly, hardly any of the actors in democracy promotion and support today act purely 'on their own' or in isolation; rather they act in networks closely aligned to and dependent on each other, where power structures and money flows also affect the nature of activities of actors. As will be seen in the final section of this chapter, and as following chapters will unpack, the relations between actors are characterized by relationships of power. Democracy promotion is not always *simply* about emancipating individuals or societies from authoritarian controls. There are constraints and power structures embedded in the way in which democracy promotion itself is designed and implemented. For example, as Chapter 5 argues, some civil society actors are more equal than others in relation to democracy promoters and their instruments.

Key foreign policy actors

The core 'foreign policy actors' and donors in the democracy support field are made up by the core Western states in the international system – the US, the UK,

France, Germany, Sweden and the Netherlands. Besides these state actors important international organizations are now actively involved in democracy support: notably the EU and the UN, as well as the OECD and, in muted forms, even some regional organizations such as the Organization of American States (OAS). Let us examine the activities of some of these actors in more detail. What do they do to support democracy and how? The obvious starting point is the US democracy support machine.

US and other Western states

The US actions in democracy support take place through various different govern-mental agencies. The core actors and instruments associated with the US support for democracy are: the US State Department, the Millennium Challenge Corp-oration (MCC) and the United States Agency for International Development (USAID).

The US State Department's role is mostly involved in making judgments on high 'diplomatic' level engagements with countries where democracy and human rights are considered at risk. Its role is to ensure that democracy and human rights are a part and parcel of US foreign policy agenda and that these values also emanate in US's engagements with third countries. It is specifically the Bureau for Democracy, Human Rights and Labor (DRL) in the State Department which is tasked with the development of democracy and human rights policy. Various pressures of course are exerted on the activity of the DRL, which has to be able to fit in the issues of democracy into US policy making on trade and security. Indeed, it is important to remember that democracy promotion never acts in a vacuum, but in the context of wider foreign policy making. When the US decides to act on democracy, this action has to be compatible with its sectional thinking on other foreign policy goals. How these relationships shape out rely in large part on the work done within the DRL. This tension between values and interests in US foreign policy is illustrated by the DRL's definition of democracy promotion. DRL insists on the purpose of democracy promotion, which is to 'create a more secure, stable, and prosperous global arena in which the United States can advance its national interests.' According to the Bureau itself,

> democracy is the one national interest that helps to secure all the others. Democratically governed nations are more likely to secure the peace, deter aggression, expand open markets, promote economic development, protect American citizens, combat international terrorism and crime, uphold human and worker rights, avoid humanitarian crises and refugee flows, improve the global environment, and protect human health. (US Department of State 2011)

The DRL therefore seems to link the promotion of democratic and human rights with the state's security and economic interests – but interestingly, seems to grant democracy a dominating status in the hierarchy of national interests.

Yet, the US democracy promotion policy is not reliant on what happens in discussions in the DRL. There are also specific 'instruments' of democracy promotion, which the US government funds and manages, the Millennium Challenge Corporation being one such instrument. This is a relatively new conditionality mechanism intimately attached to the US's development and democracy support framework. Its aim is to incentivize third countries to democratize through the tying of development aid funds to governance criteria set for these countries. Its role is to push developing states towards democratic governance reform through offering them the carrot of increased development aid according to clear and transparent criteria of measurement of democratic progress (MCC, 2007). This instrument will be examined in more detail in Chapter 5. There are other regional programmes and instruments within US foreign policy making that also contribute to the US effort to international democratization. Thus, for example, the Middle East Partnership Initiative (MEPI) programme responsible for Middle East policy has embedded within it democracy-enhancement goals and tools.

The USAID – the US's development aid delivery organization – has also assumed important responsibilities for democracy support: it has as its main function the delivery of democracy-related grass roots development aid and accounts for 80 per cent of US democracy assistance. Rather than focusing on incentivizing state elites through diplomacy or conditionality, the focus of USAID action is on delivery of democracy-related project funding to target countries: either in the form of civil society support or in the form of more extensive state-run projects. In either case the locus of emphasis is on developing grass roots oriented democracy assistance projects, which are characterized by local ownership of the projects on the ground. USAID runs its projects by opening up for tender particular sets of specialty fields, and it implements and monitors its projects from field-based offices in recipient countries.

The actions of the US government then are wide-ranging and significant. Through these various mechanisms, the US government places a considerable amount of money into democracy support – the 2013 foreign assistance budget request was $32 billion, of which $2.8 billion were dedicated to democracy, human rights, and governance – and, crucially, through its diplomatic initiatives in the State Department and the Office of the President, has historically tended to place a considerable emphasis on the importance of democracy and human rights as a condition of fruitful cooperation with countries. This is not to say that its actions have also not contravened such principles – as will be discussed in detail in later chapters – but crucially, the US has in place a significant infrastructure for promotion of democracy as a foreign policy objective and as a core characteristic of its development aid.

However, it should also be noted that the US is by no means the only player active in the field. Not only do other Western states – Canada, the UK, France, Germany, Sweden and the Netherlands most notably – see democracy as a key aspect of their foreign policy agendas in relation to developing countries, but they also put their money where their mouth is and provide a significant amount of aid to democracy assistance, rule of law and capacity-building projects. They all have slightly different focal points in delivery of aid: for example, Sweden focuses on civil society and the Netherlands on multi-party democracy development. They have then developed specific niches for themselves in democracy aid, as have new emerging central and eastern European states, most notably Poland and the Czech Republic (for more detail see Petrova 2011). The FRIDE's (2010a) extensive study of the activities of different states in democracy promotion is an invaluable tool in gaining a detailed understanding of the activities of different national states in democracy promotion today.

Box 2.1 Sweden

Sweden is one of the core countries involved in democracy support; it is one of the only countries to have truly focused on mainstreaming democracy assistance into its foreign policy and development aid systems and has done so in a deep-running and innovative manner. In its foreign policy structures it created in 2007 a specific post of Ambassador for Democracy to reflect these commitments. The implementer of much of Swedish development aid is Swedish International Development Cooperation Agency (SIDA), its development aid organization. Within SIDA sits the Department for Democracy, Human Rights and Gender Equality, responsible for the administration of Swedish democracy aid. In 2008 the total amount contributed to democracy aid was, according to Fundación para las Relaciones Internacionales y el Diálogo Exterior (FRIDE), EUR 295 million 'corresponding to 21 per cent of SIDA's budget, making this the largest category of Swedish development assistance in budgetary terms' (FRIDE 2012). Indeed, in comparison to most other actors in the field, and given its relatively small economy, Sweden is one of the most generous funders of democracy aid in the world and a leader in pushing this agenda onto the global scene.

    Unlike some of the other actors who focus on Latin America (e.g. Canada), the bulk of Swedish assistance goes to African countries (36 per cent in 2008 in fact; see FRIDE 2012). Also, unlike other countries which focus more on good governance and accountability projects (UK) or rule of law and anti-corruption and parliamentary support (the Netherlands), the focus of Swedish action is primarily on civil society work. Its core aim is to encourage democratization agents, which are seen as essential to successful democratization. Sweden has also been active in pushing for a close link to be acknowledged between democracy and development work; pushing this agenda in 2009 within the EU context, for example. The Swedish political foundations are also known notably for their actions in the field of democratization. The role of the Olof Palme Institute, for example, has been notable in the advancement of 'social' democratization in third countries through its volunteer- and dialogue-based exchanges.

An interesting question today, in the context of financial crisis and the relative decline of Western states in the face of the so-called emerging BRIC states (Brazil, Russia, India, China), is whether other countries outside of the classical democracy-promoting Western countries should today engage in democracy support. While much called for, a recent review of BRICs and democracy support reveals that little interest is shown by Brazil and India to decisively advance democracy (Carothers and Youngs 2011). What about the not so straightforwardly 'democratic' actors? China tends to fund investments in third countries without traditional conditionality interests in democracy. Russia, on the other hand, has aimed to support an alternative approach to governance in its neighbourhood. The Russian call for 'sovereign democracy' has involved the emphasis on sovereignty of states and the appreciation of the unique post-Soviet cultural space in democratization. Whether this counts as autocracy rather than democracy support is a good question (Burnell 2011). However, on the whole, the core democracy supporters remain Western states.

International organizations

In addition to state-based democracy promotion activities, various international organizations also have a key role to play in the work of democracy promotion. At least three key sets of international organizations have important roles: the EU, the UN and IFIs.

The EU does a great deal to protect democratic rights and funds various democracy assistance projects as part of its developing foreign policy arm. Thus, not only are individual member states within the EU active in democracy support, but the EU has also developed centralized 'EU-level' instruments for democracy support overseen by the EU Commission and related structures. The European External Action Service – the EU's foreign policy service – has the most direct responsibility for dealing with democracy in third countries. It is now a formalized responsibility within the EU's foreign affairs service for it to deal with democracy and human rights issues. Here, much as in the US State Department, the emphasis of activity tends to be on developing and coordinating high level diplomatic responses to democratization developments around the world; as well as on making sure that there is consistency and coordination within the work of EU's various democracy-related instruments.

Within the Commission more widely, however, there are many further instruments directly tied to democracy support. Thus, not only is there a special 'Governance Tranche' which democratizing countries can benefit from, but also civil society instruments are now in place. Thus, for example, the European Instrument for Democracy and Human Rights (EIDHR), the EU's civil society funding instrument tied to its development aid programmes and managed by the Directorate Générale (DG) Development and EuropeAid, plays a key role in distributing money to democracy and human rights projects across the EU's third country activities. The focus here is on developing grass roots responses through calls for proposals for democracy and human rights related projects (Kurki 2011). Another important instrument in civil society assistance is the European Endowment for Democracy (EED). This instrument was initially agreed upon by member states in 2012 and is in the process of being implemented in 2013 and 2014. Its role is to provide independent, flexible and non-partisan support for a variety of democracy actors in countries around the world. As the mission statement of the EED states: 'The European Endowment for Democracy will advance and encourage '"deep and sustainable democracy" in transition countries and in societies struggling for democratization, with initial, although not exclusive focus, on the European Neighbourhood' (EED 2013).

The European Neighbourhood Policy (ENP) too has as its core function promotion of democracy. The ENP, drawing on the EU's successfully democratization-creating enlargement policy, is to bring to the neighbours a respect for 'shared values' of democracy and human rights. Thus, a condition of action plans and successful development of neighbourly relations, including further trade integration, is the respect for democracy and human rights.

A unique aspect of the EU's democracy support framework is its engagement with democracy through trade. As part of its development and trade policy the EU did, with the Cotonou Agreement in 2000, make a commitment to inclusion of democratic conditionality clauses as part of its trade agreements. The aim was to ensure that the EU promotes democracy through trade as well as more overt political instruments.

In analysis of democracy support, the UN has gradually become an essential actor. Steadily enlarging its portfolio of activities, and more specifically adding peace-building operations – including support to democratic polities and institutions in countries undergoing political transition from autocracy – to its traditional peacekeeping activities, the UN has developed an array of democracy assistance instruments. With its most recent addition, the Democracy Fund (UNDEF), the UN has sought for itself a core role in democracy support in target countries. Its funding is wide-ranging and its definition ideologically open and inviting to various sets of actors. This funding is generally focused on supporting civil society, human rights activists and rule of law projects in Africa, Asia and Latin America. Its voluntarily funded contributions come from 36 nations of the UN (a fairly limited range of UN member countries then), which includes amongst the usual suspects also India, an emerging democracy funder. Nevertheless, at 110 million USD in 2010, the budget of the UNDEF is relatively small.

We must not, however, forget the role of other organizations involved in democracy support – organizations whose activities have been more covert. Notably the role of IFIs in democracy support is often overlooked. The IFIs – The World Bank and IMF for example – have an important role in democracy support. This is because they wish to encourage growth and development in target countries and crucially, in order to do so, need to encourage correct types of governance changes within the countries. From declining a role in 'political' governance support, the IFIs have moved towards (rather paradoxically, given their purely economic mandates) an increasingly active governance and anti-corruption support, which seeks to ensure that accountable, transparent and efficient bureaucracies and civil societies come to being. Such reforms are seen as part and parcel of successful development and growth reform. Economic development today depends on governance reform. The World Bank's 2007 Governance and Anti-Corruption strategy has been one key sign of the move into this field by the IFIs.

Their actions involve both conditionality instruments and more participatory grass roots projects. A crucial aspect of the IMF's support to target countries is that the targets accept the need to reform their public sector, pensions and social security structures. At the same time World Bank assists the civil societies in these countries as they see an important role for them in facilitating macro-economic reform in a consensual and efficient manner. Poverty Reduction Strategy process, for example, demands that social forces of civil society are consulted as to the nature and speed of reforms implemented. IFIs, in so doing, aim to encourage democratic reforms hand in hand with economic reforms. Other economic actors, the OECD for example, also see themselves as involved in such processes.

'Conductors' of democracy support

As we have seen, multiple state and international organizations are involved in democracy support. Through conditionality structures and direct state reform programmes they seek to push target countries towards reform. Yet, more often than not, the activities of these actors tend to be involved in the *funding* of democratization programmes. Much of democracy support today is *conducted* by a set of organizations which specialize in democracy support and in so doing offer their services to the core donors as the deliverers or conductors of democracy aid. They build democracy on the ground by implementing donor policies and funding programmes. They are not tools of coercion but of consent-based democracy building. Let us look at some of these intermediary 'conductor' organizations in more detail.

The NED is an extremely important 'independent' democracy support organization. It is funded by the US Congress but remains independent of the US State Department and foreign policy. Its key role is to guard democracy promotion globally and to bring it about in various country contexts through funding of seminars and projects, and specific civil society organizations seen as strategically important for democratization. It is a controversial organization historically as it has been seen to be directly the defender of US interests (Robinson 1996). Yet, the NED is formally independent of the US government, and much of its funding is distributed through the four affiliated institutes. Two of these are associated with the key political parties within the US: the National Democratic Institute and the International Republican Institute (IRI). The NED also encapsulates Solidarity Center, which seeks to foster effective independent trade unions in target countries, and Center for International Private Enterprise (CIPE), an institute which encourages liberal economic reform. This means that the NED can claim to be pluralistic and open in its support for various aspects of democratization and various different (American) traditions of thought on democracy – a claim, however, that has been challenged by many commentators on US democracy support (and one which we return to in Chapter 6).

Less controversial conductors of aid are the UK's Westminster Foundation and the Dutch Netherlands Institute for Multi-party Democracy (NIMD). Yet, their role is much the same. They fund – with government support – a selection of projects and actors which they see as essential to democracy. A range of activities are funded, from civil society work, to rule of law projects, to local governance and party-building projects.

Another non-partisan organization and one which has a great role in democracy support today is the Sweden-based International IDEA. It is an inter-governmental institution – run and funded by a conglomeration of 25 states – but specializes in NGO-type intermediary activity in knowledge provision and technical assistance to democratizers around the world. It is a neutral and technical expertise centre for those writing their constitutions, gender equality policies and party political systems. It specializes in constitution building, electoral processes, political participation (including issues of gender) and development-democracy link. It is highly regarded by both the donors, who turn to it for help around the world, but also by many recipients who prefer its technical and non-partisan approach and affiliation. Indeed, one of its key aims has been to work as an organization that brings together academics and practitioners, different agencies, donors and actors on the ground. While its total budget is relatively small (US$17.5 million in 2008) it is an influential and well-thought-of core actor in the field engaging in much advising and training of democracy-promotion professionals. It is distinctive in its adoption of an explicitly broad and non-procedural notion of democracy as its guiding reference point.

Besides these organizations a key set of actors in democracy support are the political foundations. Many unfamiliar with democracy support forget the crucial role of these conductor organizations, from within which democracy support initially arose. Yet, their role globally is extremely important. Not only do most European states funnel much of their democracy assistance through these organizations, but their unique standing as locally based and politically attuned actors makes them uniquely suited to negotiating the complex intermediary environment between key donors and 'local recipients'. While some claim that home state interests are defended through the actions of these foundations, their role also seems to be unquestioned in advancement of specific and locally attuned projects of democracy support. The foundations through their field offices tend to know the local context well and be able to work with suitable and trustworthy partners. This knowledge and expertise is of crucial importance to the donors, who often lack direct access or knowledge of target country contexts. The key donors are then in a sense reliant on the foundations and party political institutes to deliver many of their programmes and projects.

Besides these actors, there is now a multiplicity of network organization actors which seek to represent the interests of intermediaries or recipients in the donor field. Thus, in the EU context the role of the European Network of Political Foundations (ENoP) and the European Partnership for Democracy (EPD) are crucial to note. Another network organization of rising significance is arguably the World Movement for Democracy. The role of these organizations is to bring together democracy promotion actors and, in part, to lobby for changes in donor structures that benefit their activities. It is these organizations which most actively show the nature of the democracy support industry today: it is a highly professionalized field where NGOs and INGOs are tightly networked and keen to cooperate with donors. Indeed, the intermediary organizations are aware of their roles in democracy support and safe-guard the interests of the appropriate communities of democracy-promotion actors accordingly. Indeed, in a global industry of democracy promotion it is partially the role of such networks to defend the interests of those they represent. The democracy support industry constitutes a global whole in which key donors, states, development agencies, and NGOs and INGOs are tightly linked to each other. As we will see in later chapters, this has some crucial consequences for the construction of hegemonic ideas and practices in the field.

Box 2.2 Friedrich Ebert Stiftung

The Friedrich Ebert Stiftung (FES) is one of the oldest political foundations to engage in democracy support. It is affiliated to the Social Democratic Party and has, since 1925, engaged in civic education within Germany and since the 1960s in democratization of states in Europe and beyond. It has offices in more than 90 countries and has well-developed links to local social democratic actors in multiple contexts – not least in Greece and Portugal where it was active during their democratization.

The majority of the funds of the FES come from the German Federal State (~90 per cent) and the rest from Länder or other funders. Much of the democracy- and development-oriented funding comes through the German Development Agency. Its focal points are civil and public education and public dialogue encouragement alongside raising awareness and knowledge about global injustice and gender inequality. Indeed, the social democratic orientation of the work of the FES is still important and it remains committed to social democratic just democratization.

It works, like many Stiftungen, in cooperation with movements on the ground in various different locales. Through its close contacts with country and regional contexts, the FES's actions have been effective in bringing about positive change, although it has been – alongside other foundations – accused of defending the interests of the German state over and above its political mission (FRIDE 2010b).

Delivery of democracy promotion

But how and by who is democracy aid – a crucial constituent of democracy support – actually delivered on the ground? We cannot here cover all the diverse range of organizations, NGOs and foundations active in the democracy field. Yet, we need to appreciate some of the core differences of roles in activity of the many actors involved in the delivery. This is because the actors relate to, and work with, different sets of donors and instruments, which in part structure their aims and work.

In conditionality-based programmes, the key deliverers are country specialists or negotiators. By pushing through particular treaty agreements they enforce on the recipient state officials and bureaucrats a set of democratic commitments. Thus, bureaucrats and state officials on the donor side and the recipient side are sometimes both the local 'democracy support' deliverers and recipients. The same applies for parliamentary support programmes: here it is exchanges between parliamentarians in the West and their counterparts in developing countries that form the core of the interaction and 'aid'.

Yet, in the case of civil society oriented support the situation is somewhat different. Here the core deliverers and recipients of aid are NGOs as well as private companies, the two main categories of actors on the ground involved in implementation of democracy projects. Besides them various think tanks, educational institutions, gender rights groups and service delivery NGOs receive funding from western democracy promoters.

NGOs involved in democracy support range from those which represent human rights organizations to those specializing in civil society activism. Increasingly various child and gender support NGOs are receiving money under the auspices especially of the EU's more 'developmentally' oriented democracy support structures. These NGOs sometimes involve political foundations, which however, more often than not, act as conductors of aid by 'subcontracting' local NGOs on the ground – from church associations to local human rights or service-delivery NGOs.

Think tanks too receive a considerable amount of input – from pro-business think tanks, such as CIPE, to anti-globalization groups such as Third World Network. Universities and education institutions also receive money from democracy support programmes to run civic education and human rights training and degrees. Trade unions have received rather small contributions from the EU as the EU has recently acknowledged, but in the US context the American Center for International Labour Solidarity (or Solidarity Center) is familiar with working with trade unions.

Rather more surprising is the role of private companies in democracy support (see Box 2.3). Yet, if we bear in mind the 'privatization' and 'outsourcing' trends in modern governance, this is far from unexpected. Their role, mostly in the US context, is to supply to the market of democracy aid provision with efficient and value-for-money democracy assistance projects and programmes. It is these companies – Chemonics, DAC and others – that most democracy aid actually runs through.

Box 2.3 Chemonics

Chemonics is an example of one of the private firms engaged in democracy support today. Operating primarily in the increasingly privatized American context, one of its core missions is to deliver a selection of USAID and government-funded democracy and governance projects. As an international development consultancy firm its role is, in its own words to: 'design and implement projects in financial services, private sector development, health, environmental management, gender, conflict and disaster management, democracy and governance, and agriculture' (Chemonics 2012a). They work under contract for USAID and take on projects in various fields from micro-finance to agriculture, forestry and governance projects; as well as advocating in general, or lobbying for, the continued recognition of the importance of development funding. They are a 'for-profit firm' and have at their core aims 'excellence and value' (Chemonics 2012b). They claim expertise in efficient solutions and 'participative' approach to development as well as providing effective measurement of the success of programmes. Their results, it is to be noted, are measured primarily in economic terms of improving growth or access to markets of core sets of actors (Chemonics 2012c).

In the democracy field, Chemonics argues that it 'offers a range of services, from e-government to building civil society's capacity to serve as a watchdog' (Chemonics 2012a). The aim is to make sure legitimacy of governance is improved through defences of individual freedoms. It is emphasized that, while differing contexts demand different solutions on the ground, the goals are the same: 'a host-nation environment that respects individual liberty, guarantees transparent government institutions, and gives average individuals a real voice in their futures regardless of race, gender, ethnicity, familial origin, political affiliation, personal opinion, or economic status' (Chemonics 2012a). Working to reduce corruption and incentivize through competition civil society actors to engage positively with development and democracy (interest representation specifically – see e.g. Program Representasi Project) Chemonics also works on 'the laws, regulations, policies, and processes that guide interaction with government institutions and build independent oversight mechanisms' (Chemonics 2012a).

The work of Chemonics, encapsulating at present nine Democracy and Governance projects, demonstrates amply the role of private firms in the delivery of democracy aid. Striking here is the 'commodification' of the idea of democracy promotion: the delivery to specific markets of a specific product on the basis of local market research.

Reflections on power relations between democracy actors

As we will see, a critical approach to democracy promotion introduces questions of power, conceptualization and of consensus and hegemony. It asks us to reflect on analytical questions often sidelined in purely descriptive or instrumental accounts of democracy promotion. Sure, democracy promotion is a more global industry today – this is an important empirical fact, yet to be fully understood by many critics, including critical theorists, of democracy promotion. But globalization of activity does not of course mean that power relations of democracy promotion have disappeared. Just because it is no longer simply the US promoting democracy in its own national interests, this does not mean interests and power do not play a role in it. We need to then ask: If democracy promotion is now done by a multiplicity of actors, where does the power lie in democracy promotion today? Are some actors more important than others, or do they act in a 'level playing field'? What conceptions of democracy are promoted by the different actors and why? Is there consensus and cooperation between the different actors or are there actually somewhat different aims directing their actions?

While some of these questions cannot be addressed fully here and thus remain to be explored in the chapters that follow, let us here reflect on the global nature of democracy promotion and what it seems to suggest with regard to power relations between actors in the field of democracy promotion. We examine two aspects of these power-relations: 1) material distribution of means in democracy promotion; and 2) power to define meaning of democracy and what its promotion involves.

If democracy promotion today is a global industry, is it a level playing field? It seems that this is not the case. Relations of power between democracy donors, and between democracy donors, conductors and recipients, remain and structure the field of democracy promotion. Arguably the key donors – the US, EU and IFIs perhaps most notably – hold considerable financial power in democracy promotion: because many of the funds for democracy promotion emanate from these donors, their role is disproportionate in being able to 'direct' if not 'dictate' the kinds of activities that other actors – NGOs, political foundations or private actors – should be engaged in. Thus, what can be observed today in the democracy promotion field are relations of financial power which come to relate to power over content of democracy promotion. If the USAID sets up a programme on a specific kind of civil society engagement, it is the NGOs which need to respond to this call by adapting their activities in such ways as to be able to bid for this programmatic money. There are relations of power in the bidding processes of democracy aid, which we will turn to in more detail in Chapters 4 and 5.

These actors also have great power in structuring the field of development and democracy promotion assistance more generally. The IFIs have a disproportionate role here. The kinds of activities and relationships between donors and the recipients that are fostered have effects on other actors. When IFIs moved to good governance and anti-corruption work, most other donors, even US and EU took their cue from the activities set out here. The kinds of diagnostics for identification of good governance, accountability and development that are worked with, also deeply influence the work of the US and EU as well as other state and international organizations in the development field. It is not the case then that all kinds of management tools or programmes are possible, but rather it is the case that some tools and foci are 'in fashion', and this is often the case because they are favoured by the key donor actors. As a result NGOs and political foundations, while important delivery organizations, need to adjust to the field of donor activities in setting up their approaches to democratization.

This raises the question of 'what is promoted'? As suggested in the introduction to this chapter, relations between democracy promotion actors are also relationships of power. This is also revealed in part by a closer examination of 'what is promoted'. From a critical angle, one of the key concerns with regard to democracy promotion is a concern over 'what kinds of democracy' are promoted. So what is promoted by these actors we have outlined?

A recent study of the conceptual foundations of various actors' conceptions of democracy indicates that a broadly 'liberal democratic' framework dominates in how key donors and even conductors and implementers of democracy aid conceptualize democracy, and thus 'ideal models of governance' promoted in countries. The US's democracy promotion is most straightforwardly for the promotion of liberal democratic governance: elections, liberal constitutionalism, liberal entrepreneurial civil society and open markets. The EU's democracy promotion is also liberal democratic in its core, though fuzzy around the edges. The IFIs promote what is described as an 'embedded neoliberal model of democracy': one which places open market economies at the heart of thinking on democracy, while ensuring that flanking measures are in place to make sure that liberal democratic and economic systems are 'stable' (Kurki 2013).

Interestingly, these more or less liberal democratic models of governance are by and large accepted nowadays by the NGOs and political foundations (Kurki 2013). This is despite the fact that historically some of these conductors and recipients of democracy aid actually have had in mind models of democracy that are drastically or marginally different from those usually characterized as 'liberal democratic' (many political foundations have explicitly promoted social democracy or even radical models of democracy, and some NGOs have in the past explicitly argued against the liberal democratic dogma in democratizing and liberalizing countries). However, today, many NGOs and foundations have aligned their conceptual foundations with the 'consensus' on liberal democracy, emanating from key donors. This has crucial consequences for democracy promotion in target states for if liberal democracy is now the only model of democracy that can be promoted, this means that domestic power relations in societies and their relations to international actors and interests have become very particular. Liberal democracy is an ideological model which is but one amongst many and as such which results, not in equalization of power relations, but specific kinds of power relations between economy and politics, and between different socio-economic groups in society. With this in mind, it seems that the global industry of democracy promotion today may be more of a tool of specific ideological thinking than it is a truly global industry where all views of democracy and how it should relate to the economy are aired, discussed and promoted. We will return to these issues in the following chapters.

Conclusion

As we have seen, a considerable variety of actors are involved in democracy support today. It is no longer a foreign policy agenda undertaken merely by the US but involves a whole variety of actors locked into relations of dependency and cooperation. It is in such a context that the dynamics of power are negotiated. The democracy promotion industry fosters within it both ideological hegemonic projects and material power structures, which we need to appreciate in more detail to get a sense of what democracy support today is about – on the ground and in its effects on target societies and the donors. It is analysis of these dynamics that we now move to.

Note

1.   This budget is small compared to the budget lines of some of the major actors, e.g. the US and the EU, but the core activity of UNDEF is to finance small civil society organizations working on implementing small-scale projects (from 50,000 USD to 500,000 USD) that deliver quick and high impact results. Thus, despite the small budget, arguably the UNDEF actually plays a very significant role in supporting local civil society organizations.

3   Is democracy promotion about defence of values or about the safeguarding of interests?

One of the key questions that has haunted democracy promotion from the start, and continues to haunt it today in the context of the Arab Spring, has been the implication that when democracy is promoted this is merely done because it is in the interests of democracy promoting actors. Usually, when such criticisms are voiced, it is the Western democracy-promoting states that are seen as the key beneficiaries of democracy aid, however 'altruistic' the rhetoric of democracy promotion or support might be.

This chapter revisits this claim and argues that democracy promotion today can, and should, be understood as an agenda where interests and values are tied together in complex sets of ways. Certainly, interest calculations do play a role in democracy promotion – it would be foolish to expect they did not. However, this does not mean that values, of democracy, liberty or emancipation from power cannot and do not emanate from democracy promotion policies, actions and rhetoric. Indeed, they do: we find that when we examine the question of interests and values from a critical perspective, we can observe that interests are tied in complex ways to value systems of democracy promotion and vice versa, but from this perspective we can also come to somewhat more nuanced understandings of the complex interplay of values and interests. We will show that the values in democracy promotion are such that they coincide with some interests more than others; and interests are such that they coincide with some value systems rather than others.

Moreover, we also trace here how, in the era of 'globalized' democracy promotion in which international organizations and NGOs (surveyed in Chapter 2) also play a part alongside key state actors, the interests of actors often come through in democracy promotion in an increasingly *indirect* manner. Management instruments of civil society aid, neutral techniques of good governance and best practices of democratic engagement can all be infused with power: and, as a result, defend some values and interests more than others. Indeed, we suggest here that in a more globalized industry of democracy promotion it may be in part because of implicit 'coincidences of interests' that democracy promotion ends up supporting some kinds of political and economic orders rather than others, and thus may become a tool of hegemony (issue examined in more detail in Chapter 7). A critical approach is particularly well-placed to open our eyes to these hidden forms of power, interest and values in democracy promotion today.

At the same time, value agendas may today also reflect tendencies towards curious forms of 'hollow hegemony' where both interests and values are less clear than before. This is why studying complex and fascinating inter-connections between values and interests is important. Simplistic formulas such as 'democracy promotion is about Western state interests' fail to grasp the full and interesting relations of values and interests.

This chapter will examine some of the key positions on interests and values. We examine first the optimistic liberal interpretations where values and interests are contrasted, but then move on to show that even most liberal and realist thinkers today would perceive values and interests as mutually supportive, rather than as clashing sets of concerns. Because we find these formulations somewhat unclear, however, we then examine some of the more interesting critical theoretical tools for understanding values and interests in democracy promotion. These we hope resolve some key issues about how values and interests interact, as well as point us towards new sites and forms of interaction between interest and value.

Arguments about interests, and defenders of 'altruistic' democracy promotion

> The world must be made safe for democracy. Its peace must be planted upon the tested foundations of political liberty. We have no selfish ends to serve. We desire no conquest, no dominion. We seek no indemnities for ourselves, no material compensation for sacrifices we shall freely make. We are but one of the champions of the rights of mankind. We shall be satisfied when those rights have been made as secure as the faith and the freedom of nations can make them.
>
> Woodrow Wilson, War Message, 2 April 1917

Wilson's war message demonstrates not only the value-principled commitment of key democracy promoters to the idea of democracy, but also the strongly held belief that it is not self-interest that is served by this end, but rather the interests of all 'free men'. Such statements of 'altruistic' promotion of democracy and freedom may find purchase, on occasion, amongst policy-makers even today. When such assumptions are made, it is as if democracy promotion was a religious or unearthly cause to which benign and enlightened actors commit themselves for the sake of 'saving' the world of its ills and troubles.

Yet, such assumptions of *pure* altruism are relatively rare today in democracy promotion. Both practitioners and academics have long accepted that interests as well as values play a role in directing democracy promotion: how it is done, when it is done and whether it is done in specific places and at specific times. Democracy promoters cannot afford to, nor would benefit from, acting or appearing to act as God-like declarers of truth and righteousness, as crusaders for pure good. Democracy promotion is a policy which is pursued in the context of wider foreign policy or programmatic aims, which famously have wider aims: often the defence of the interests of the state and its population in terms of security, wealth and stability. Such 'interest-concerns' do and must intervene and interact with the aims and methods of democracy promotion.

Yet, this does not mean that democracy promotion is entirely interest-driven – a claim that some critics of democracy promotion make. Critics often point out that democracy promoters only intervene when it is in their interests; when democracy promotion is made to serve other ends, when it is instrumental in the defence of interests of the states, conceived in terms of security, wealth or stability. The interest-driven nature of democracy promotion is cited as the cause of the obvious inability of democracy promoters to consistently defend the principles they advocate. Thus, for example, it is pointed out that while democracy is promoted in Iraq or Libya, Chile in the 1980s or Saudi Arabia today did not seem to warrant the same level of concern with regard to democratic rights and beliefs as other states. This, it is argued, is because democracy promoters only intervene when it is in their interests to do so; when democracy intervention serves other ends: security needs, trade aims or energy policy.

These positions mark, if you like, the end points of a continuum of views. As such, neither is persuasive as a general stance – although some rare cases of purely interest-driven and purely value-driven democracy promotion may be identifiable. As a result, to narrow debate on values and interests to a debate between two crude positions such as these would be foolish, and will lead us to misunderstand the complex and interesting interconnections between values and interests in democracy promotion.

To gain a better sense of what the relationship between values and interests might be in democracy promotion far more sophisticated stances are needed. How may we think of value and interest agendas as interacting? Let's review some of the key positions we could take on the issue of interest and values and evaluate the significance of these positions for our understanding of the relationship between foreign policy agendas of key actors and the 'value' of promoting democracy. These more sophisticated understandings also exist somewhere on the continuum we have established, but can be positioned closer to the middle parts of the continuum.

Liberal value-optimists

The 'optimists', who err on the side of value-driven arguments rather than interest-driven ones, can build their arguments on the value-interest question in (at least) two distinct ways.

First, they may argue that even self-interested actors can and will promote values when opportunities present themselves. This may mean that even if democracy or human rights are not always the only or the overriding interests, they are ones which can be promoted to a significant extent independent of interest consider-ations. As Wilson states, principles can be promoted because they are right, not because they serve other ends. There is 'room' in international politics for values and principles, and in the right contexts and through the right kinds of methods they can be advanced. Liberal internationalists believe that, when assessed with reason and caution and advanced in correct circumstances, core liberal principles can incrementally be spread in the international system in ways which find 'niches' for value-principles of democracy and liberty to flourish. In so doing, in the long run, they will come to render international politics more peaceful and serene.

Yet, second, a liberal optimist belief may not need to rely on creating 'room' for altruistic actions. Liberal optimists can also specifically align their value-principles with interest agendas. Indeed, in recent years some of these liberal optimists have explicitly come to the view that principles of democracy and human rights can actually be productively embedded in 'interest agendas'. That is, when democracy and human rights are promoted, they are consistent with and complement interest-driven security or energy agendas. Thus, for example, the War on Terror associated the promotion of democracy as a value with the interest of global security. Democracies were seen as instrumentally beneficial for security, as well as, simultaneously, desirable in their own right.

Liberal internationalism and the so-called liberal democratic peace theory arguably are also underpinned by these kinds of concerns. It is not the case that, for liberal internationalists or advocates of democratic peace, democracy is advanced because it is in and of itself 'good'. For many liberals it is advanced because it is in the interests of the Western states: because of the peace-creating, stability-engendering and wealth-spreading functions democratization plays. Democracy is advanced because it is in the security and stability interests of liberal democratic actors in the system today. There is nothing altruistic per se then about this agenda; except in the sense that interests can be seen as aligned to specific values, such as democracy and liberty, which are considered in line with interests identified.

These positions are important and, it can be claimed, underpin much of the practice and policy-making on democracy promotion. Many practitioners believe that democracy promotion is compatible with altruistic ends and also simultaneously with instrumental interest agendas. Promotion of democracy is then the best of both worlds: it advances values that are universally correct and agendas which benefit Western and non-Western actors. In this sense, as some have pointed out, democracy promotion does seem to assume – even on the question of interests and values – that 'all good things go together' (Freyburg *et al.* 2012).

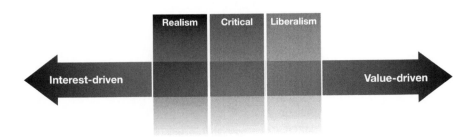

Figure 3.1 Values–interests continuum

Yet, such liberal 'middle positions' are not the only ones we should consider, and are in fact considered problematic by many. Realists, as well as Gramscian critics, take exception to the optimistic readings of the values-interest question by 'liberal' commentators.

Realist critics

Realist commentators point out that the US government, or the EU for that matter, has had no scruples about funding and assisting, and condoning, regimes which have consistently violated human rights and democratic principles. Whether it is support to Chile, Nicaragua or Egypt, Western policy-makers, when their interests are so served, will happily stand by authoritarian leaders and do little if anything in defence of democratic rights and principles. Indeed, political liberalization messages tend to be watered down as democratic rights and interests do not take precedence over fundamental security and economic interests that organize the relationship between liberal democracies and the authoritarian regimes they support. It does not mean that there are no efforts by democratic regimes to try to convince authoritarian regimes to gradually liberalize. Instead those government-to-government efforts are cast aside once authoritarian interlocutors agitate the threat of chaos, if they were to disappear. James A. Baker describes this dilemma when he explains that hints at political liberalization in Egypt were systematically repulsed by Hosni Mubarrak along the tune of 'it is either me or the Muslim Brotherhood'. As Baker argues:

> We have to consider principles and values, yes: democracy, human rights, freedom. But we also have to consider the national interest, whether or not the particular entity we're dealing with is aligned with the United States or not. And those two considerations meet head-on in this conflict. (James A. Baker quoted by Gwertzman 2011)

As the quote illustrates, traditional 'realist' commentators would explain this dilemma between values and interests by the predominance of 'national interest' in determination of foreign policy objectives of any state or international actor (see Hyde-Price 2008; Schweller 2000). They point to the need to consider the promotion of 'values' such as democracy and human rights in the context of the constant demand for policies which serve the interests of western actors. From this perspective, as E.H. Carr (1939) pointed out, liberal belief in value-promotion often serves to hide and disguise hypocritical agendas – and hubris of Western actors' own positions in the international order. Values become, if you like, a veneer which – even if actors truly believe in these values – comes to hide the reality in which power of the 'haves' is under the disguise of value agendas pushed upon the 'have-nots'. Values and interests may go together, but it is interest-agendas which do (and should do) the driving.

These liberal and realist positions are good at accounting for the complementary nature of values and interests. However, they do not give us a detailed explanation of how values and interests exactly come together in democracy promotion, and still assume that values and interests are essentially two separate things. A critical approach has more potential in opening up the interconnected nature of values and interests. Indeed, a variety of critical theorists have managed to provide interesting accounts of the way in which the very nature of values is shaped by interests.

Critical approach

Critical theorists, such as Robinson (1996) and Gills *et al.* (1993), have pointed to a different kind of an interest configuration in determining democracy promotion. They argue that underpinning specific 'national' policy-making decisions lay the interests of capitalist classes. Western foreign policy for them boils down to, in the end, the promotion of the interests of major capitalist groups, companies and multinational interests. Thus, to explain democracy promotion as merely being about foreign policy interests of states is not enough: it is in fact about national interest protection underpinned by capitalist interest and classes. The overall objective was, for American elites, to solidify its ideological hegemony, a hegemony founded on two pillars: liberal democracy and free market economy (a position described in more detail in Chapters 6 and 7).

Hence, Robinson argues, when US intervened in Nicaragua or the Philippines, it was essentially to establish a form of social order which benefited the interest of the US as a state in two ways. Firstly, the US became heavily involved in the internal workings of governments in its extended 'neighbourhood' in an attempt to generate states that were stable, orderly and receptive to American interests. Secondly, such interventionism was also playing in the favour of major capitalist groups who also wanted the state stable and orderly, but in a manner which facilitated the extraction of goods, materials and services from these states by the US-associated big business on the open market. It is at this juncture between political and economic interests that we find the rationale, on behalf of the US, to promote specific principles of open market, and forms of democracy compatible with these principles. It is also why particular kinds of ideas of democracy are promoted, Robinson argues.

Similar arguments have been made with regard to the promotion of democracy by the EU or other Western states. Less than high principles seem to be involved; reality verges towards protection of 'lowly self-interest' as, for example, Crawford (2008) argues in relation to democracy work in Central Asia (see also Youngs 2010; Kurki 2013).

Interestingly, it is crucial to note that Robinson's analysis suggests that it is the promotion of particular ideas about democracy's meaning, which structures social affairs in very specific ways. In this way Robinson argues *value-systems promoted are intricately tied to protection of interests through it*. Open market democracies are promoted – regardless of the politico-economic system at home – because open market democracy ensures markets for domestically produced or fostered products or investment. The very conceptions of democracy, and how democracy is related to the market, are intricately tied to particular understandings of interests.

Values and interests, Robinson's analysis then suggests, do not then 'clash' as much as they *profoundly come together*. Particular kinds of values can be promoted if they substantiate and assist in the defence of core interests. This is an important insight, and a key contribution of a critical approach. However, we argue here that even closer and more detailed attention needs to be paid to the coming together of values and interests today than that afforded by Robinson. Indeed, in the following section we argue that a close examination of the intricate tying together of values and interests today suggests that increasingly a fascinating 'coincidence' of interests and values explains the structure of democracy promotion. Crucially, we suggest below that this does not mean that 'intentional' efforts to use or direct populations to meet specific interests are at work in democracy promotion. The systematic effects of the, quite unintentional, but yet significant, forms of 'ideational shaping' through democracy support need to be appreciated in more detail.

Values and interests as 'coincidental': the (increasingly) subtle power politics of democracy support today

A key claim of this book is that commentators and observers, and the practitioners of democracy promotion, need to be aware of the interaction of interests and values, the role of interests in shaping value-judgments and forms of values and the role of values in shaping interests. This is because democracy promotion is not simply an 'instrument' of foreign policy interests but much more than this; it is a conduit and a mediator of interests and values.

Democracy promotion is a value-driven agenda; there is no doubt about that. Democracy is a normative concept with multiple possible value-laden meanings. Yet, it is not a concept with a single meaning, nor with singular power relations arising from it. Multiple forms of power and interests are played out in it and through it. Democracy promotion today does not seem to serve singular one-sided interests – of the foreign policy-makers or capitalists. Yet, from our critical perspective, it does serve interests. How? There are at least three ways in which it does.

First, even today, democracy promotion can, at times, be a rather straightforward instrument of foreign policy, and can be used as a front for seeking other aims. Thus, some have argued that, for example, in Iraq the US's aim was in fact to seek its own security and energy interests in the country and that promotion of democracy was merely a means to that end. The European Union's interactions in the neighbourhood have also been accused of being little more than rhetorical covers for a purely interest-driven push for energy access and wider markets.

The existence of such power-based evaluations seem to be particularly prevalent when 'high politics' and relations with great power rivals are at stake. For example, the shying away from meaningful democracy criticism of the Chinese state or even reluctance to engage in a serious way in Syria, are examples of hard power interests trumping value considerations. Even in high politics of 'development' rather crude realist calculations are made as to who receives budget support or other forms of development aid. Often such decisions are not made on objective and apolitical grounds as to who deserves or needs that support. It is crucial to note that while these dynamics persist, they do not entail that democracy promotion per se is a sham but rather merely that democracy promotion is never a policy agenda pursued on its own, in isolation or without wider considerations in mind. Yet this, relatively straightforward value-interest interaction is not the only way in which values and interests interplay today.

Second, it may be quite possible for practitioners and policy-makers – even in the case of challenging high politics cases – to believe in the rhetoric and values which they promote and in the universality and necessity of the promotion of such ideals. Our research suggests that in the democracy promotion industry today many practitioners do firmly believe in the superiority of the values they promote and thus the push for democracy advancement is not only interest-driven or trumped but value-infiltrated. Thus, the European Union pushes for neighbourhood policies – which admittedly serve their interests – because these policies are seen as superior, as 'inevitable' and as 'modern' and thus as simply both firmly in the interests of the Union but also in the interest of all others (Kurki 2013). The liberal assumption that the right values go together with mutual interests informs the policy activities it seems of many democracy promoters.

Even the NGO actors then often accept nowadays that there is no clash of values and interests but that the process of democratization is a progressive one and in the 'interests' of target publics.

Often this form of logic of course ends up becoming a little lazy in deciphering whose interests *exactly* are promoted and whether all actors in target countries benefit equally. Yet, the view that the rest of the world should abide by and, in fact, already universally commit to, liberal democratic values, institutional responses and democratic conceptions is widespread and, indeed, endemic in the democracy promotion community (Kurki 2013). Subtle coming together of interests (in liberal order) and values (of liberal democracy and liberal capitalism) takes place.

This is not all, however, for, third, even more subtle mergers of interests and values take place – often in the fascinating, and in our view increasingly important, 'low politics' of democracy promotion and support. The critical approach directs us to pay attention to the unobservable or hidden forms of power, and indeed, from such a perspective we can see that more implicit forms of democracy promotion and hidden dynamics within them play an important role in democracy promotion today. The low politics of democracy promotion and support refer to the 'technical' and 'neutral' delivery mechanisms and instruments of assistance: how democracy promotion and support is conducted on an everyday basis, outside the high diplomatic games, dialogues and considerations.

It would seem at first glance that at such a level of technical delivery of aid no specific values, and no specific interests, are implicated: this is the site of neutral technical interventions. This is not the case we argue. In fact, it is on these levels that some of the most subtle and the most interesting interplays of values and interests are to be observed.

Thus, for example, most civil society funders and funding instruments state that they do not prefer one type of actors, with a very specific set of values, over others. Thus, it is made clear that it is not only Western-friendly actors that are funded but that potentially many types of democracy promoters – from women's groups to trade unions – may receive support. These beliefs are not only communicated to the recipients but also clearly internalized by the funders and the practitioners who conduct the funding processes. The decisions are made on technical and objective grounds, not on political or value grounds per se. But does this mean that specific values or interests do not come through in such aid? It does not.

Our research has shown that even when values and interests are both removed from the equation of aid, specific kinds of value and interest assumptions can filter through into democracy promotion reality. Thus, implicitly, behind the invocations of value pluralism, it is often believed that NGOs and CSOs (civil society organizations) which receive funding must be willing to abide by the funding criteria, they must commit to efficiency of spending, reporting and auditing requirements. This in and of itself would sound reasonable, if one did not reflect on the ways in which funding management requirements – such as logical framework analysis – can impact on the nature of the work of the actors concerned. The technical requirements push CSOs towards promising activities which are easily 'observable' and 'measurable' in effects and which conform to the requirements and expectations made of 'entrepreneurial' CSO actors today. Self-confirming these assumptions means that CSOs willingly and actively conform to increasingly liberal and neoliberal assumptions. Even more radical or non-liberal democratic actors today find the pressures great to conform (Kurki 2013). We will return to this issue in Chapters 4 and 5.

In these ways, specific values can – implicitly – permeate democracy support but do so in complex and indirect ways compared to specific interests. Thus, while not overtly arguing against radical agendas or anti-Western CSO activity, the technical requirements are such that they tend to weed out these types of explicitly political, often volunteer-based organizations from funding. There is a 'co-incidence' of interests and values that emerges from the workings of such 'governmentality' techniques in global politics.

This co-incidence of interests and values is an important point to recognize, for it has an impact on how we evaluate the interests and values at work in democracy promotion today. There are some grounds to suggest that there are new modes of both values and interests at play in democracy support and that these – being more covert and in fact sometimes even unintentional – need to be better understood for the nature of democracy promotion, and its power relations, to be adequately comprehended. To assume that democracy promotion is a Western, state-driven and interest-driven project is to simplify the picture to the extreme. This is not only unhelpful in that it angers many practitioners to have their actions so misunderstood, but also it is unhelpful in terms of scholars and students being able to probe deeper into some of the more fascinating power dynamics of democracy support (and indeed global governance policy). These power relations are now often played out implicitly in technical and technocratic instruments rather than in explicit invocations of either values or interests.

The global nature of democracy promotion, examined in Chapter 2, today supports these dynamics. When democracy promotion is no longer something that is considered by the foreign ministries but an agenda which criss-crosses across policy departments (development, trade, foreign policy, security, energy), and when state actors in these fields are deeply embedded in global and international policy networks, it is harder and harder to work with the assumption that the interest of one actor or another is deeply reflective of policies of individual actors. The 'networkisation' and the resultant globalization of democracy support reflects the diffusion of this policy agenda but also, arguably, the changing nature of both interests and values in today's global politics. No longer is international politics about national interest, or even clear-cut capitalist interests. Nor is it about clear-cut values – promoted in one's interest or otherwise. Instead it is about management of global affairs under increasingly technocratic and technical instruments. This affects democracy promotion and how it functions, how it tones its value principles and how interests – and power relations – are structured through it. More subtle and complexity-sensitive approaches to study of interests and values are needed today in understanding democracy support. Singular liberal, realist or Marxist tools do not seem, on their own, to do the job in trying to get to grips with this question in democracy support today.

Beyond values and interests

With these developments in mind, another interesting perspective to consider is that proposed by David Chandler. He suggests that we need to read international policy-making today in new ways. He argues that we need to acknowledge the shift since the 1990s towards more 'value-based' international politics. Unlike during the Cold War, it is value-based foreign policies that many states and international organizations aspire to. Democracy promotion's role is a case in point: it is a value-based foreign policy which has come to organize actions of key actors. Policy agendas are 'increasingly justified in moral or value-based terms, giving legitimacy to the actions in and of themselves' (Chandler 2007: 719). However, this is not the end of the story, for Chandler introduces an important shift in how we should understand the movement towards values.

Chandler argues that we should see international value-led policy making as something which is neither a reflection of more altruistic or ideological shifts in international politics, nor as an interest-based agenda in disguise. Instead, we should see value-based foreign policy reflective of a shift towards what he calls the 'hollow hegemony', an international order where state elites are finding it increasingly difficult to articulate clear interests or agendas and as a result come to promote international 'value agendas' as guises which paradoxically hide their preference for stepping away from or avoiding taking responsibility for their own actions and thus even interests. As Chandler argues, international actors today:

> often seek to reject, rather than welcome, the responsibilities of power. Rather than claiming the rights to power, many governments seem to be

happier when they are disclaiming them, seeking to devolve policy-making responsibilities to regional and local authorities or to higher bodies such as the European Union or international institutions. There is a crisis of political legitimacy at the level of the nation-state which is at the heart of the shift away from the projection of power in the framework of national interests. This is not so much because political elites have taken up new ideas and thereby understand their interests as 'global concerns' rather than national ones, as much as the lack of an organising collective ideology. (Chandler 2007: 720)

This perspective is a provocative one for it pushes us to think even further about the values and interests and their relationship in democracy promotion agenda. Specifically, this perspective raises the prospect that it is *the lack* of clear political subjectivity, power and ideology that motivates the value-driven policy. Behind the value-laden veneer of policy making today, he suggests, there is no big agenda but rather hollowness: a lack of clear strategic, ideological or interest-driven agenda. This is what, for Chandler, explains the irrationality and *ad hoc*-ness of much of Western policy. '[P]olitical elites are keen to express the rhetoric of high moral responsibility in the international sphere but are reluctant to take responsibility for either policy-making or policy outcomes' (Chandler 2007: 721). This explains the interest in 'collective' action and intractable 'global' problems and movement of responsibility to the weak (the local, the poor) and, crucially, the focus on justifying actions in value-based rather than interest-based terms. There is both a lack of clear ideological values and clear interests in many international policy agendas. As we have suggested elsewhere, the role of liberal ideas are changing in the current world order: they are becoming less and less 'ideological'.

This perspective is provocative, but some indications of precisely these trends can be seen played out in democracy promotion today. Thus, for example, the shifts towards global, multilateral actions, local ownership, and movement towards global idealized notions of democracy which are not contested or discussed, seem to indicate the movement towards less clear-cut, less 'responsibility' based action. It is not necessarily so much the case that democracy promoters accept a responsibility to civilize or democratize – as many critics have argued – but rather that they do not. It is bureaucratized best practices, depoliticized management instruments, and value-driven logics which are fuzzy and open to different meanings, which guide action. Interestingly, our critical analysis of covert as well as overt language and beliefs of democracy promoters is consistent with the possibility that a 'hollow hegemony', rather than either a colonizing or a benign 'liberal' hegemony, may come to reign in democracy promotion today. This has important implications for what we think the role of democracy promotion is and what it can achieve, and for how democracy is interpreted by promoters and democratizers alike, issues which we will return to in Chapter 7 and the Conclusion.

Conclusion

When we analyse democracy promotion from the point of view of a critical perspective, which is attuned to both covert as well as overt forms of power, it is clear that when democracy is promoted it is not done on purely altruistic grounds. Not all states are made subject to conditionality, not all kinds of democratic actor are promoted, nor are all kinds of democracy encouraged. But this is of course today recognized by democracy promoters themselves. Interests as well as values are always close to the minds of policy makers reflecting on democracy's advocacy. Most practitioners recognize the complexity of the relationship between values and interests; which in part explains why responses to different regions and countries differ. Different interest considerations direct engagements and the ability to 'create room' for value promotion. Thus, value and interest considerations play out in different ways on different levels, or in different spheres of democracy promotion. Therefore, in high politics of democracy – in how China is talked to or which states development aid is accorded to – more overt interest considerations are played out. Even here, however, many policy-makers and practitioners continue to consider democracy's cause in the context of multiple other pressures *because* they hold a deeply-felt value commitment to the superiority of this form of governance as well as believing in its stability-inducing and progressive potential in creating a better world order. The values of liberty and democracy still play a role, and indeed often challenge and mould the ways in which interest consider-ations are even taken into account. Interest and values need not be contrastive.

Indeed, as even critical scholars have noted, specific ideas and values can carry and support – or strategically select – specific kinds of interests. This is crucial to note for this is indeed a crucial dynamic in democracy support. Thus, as Robinson has argued, the fact that specific ideals about what democracy is are passed on in democracy support, comes to have consequences for the kinds of democracy and also politico-economic order that are instituted in target states. Values promoted carry – sometimes in subtle ways – interests.

This process of diffusion, we have suggested here, has reached a new level today in democracy support. Where Robinson expected there to be a capitalist set of interests and at least partially intentional planning behind the invocation of specific value priorities, we note that things today are more complex. Indeed, with the diffusion of a global ideology of liberalism, the modes of operation of the liberal value-interest nexus are also changing. This means also that the usual perspectives on values and interests – often informed by liberal framings of how interests and values come together – may miss important dynamics in democracy promotion. While a complex set of considerations – some of them value-driven – are considered in democracy promotion today, a critical approach attuned to covert workings of power allows us to observe dynamics of power which indicate implicit forms of power construction. Technocratic and technical forms of management and instru-ments associated with these are the sites of subtle interplays of values and interests. What a critical approach can give us today then is a better appreciation of the subtle and often implicit forms of power in democracy support. Because seemingly apolitical best practices, self-management and technical requirements play much more of a role today in democracy promotion than before, the modes of power and values are also shifting. A 'small-l' liberal democratic order, with 'co-incidences of interest' seems to be the new reality of contemporary democracy support.

Note

1. James A. Baker was President Ronald Reagan's Chief of Staff (1981–85), Secretary of the Treasury (1985–88), and President George H. Bush's Secretary of State (1989–92).

4 Is democracy promotion regime change?

Whether democracy promotion is a policy that is closely linked, or even equivalent to, regime change is one of the most challenging and heated questions posed to democracy promoters today. It is a question tied to a specific historical context, however, having acquired special significance in the aftermath of the 2003 invasion and subsequent occupation of Iraq by a coalition led by the United States. Prior to this event, there was little doubt in the minds of governmental officials and practitioners of democracy promotion that their work had nothing to do with regime change. Not only was democracy promotion since 1990s an increasingly voluntary and non-coercive agenda, but also it was not justified by 'Cold War-era' security interest arguments. This all changed with the Iraq War: not only does democracy promotion become tied to the wider security interests of Western states but also coercive military methods were introduced as the final front in the fight against 'rogue states'.

The Iraq intervention, as a result, has had noticeable ramifications for democracy promotion. The association with 'regime change' through Iraq has given democracy promotion a bad name, and consequently, especially in the United States, democracy promotion as a foreign policy agenda has suffered a significant backlash (Carothers 2007a, 2008; Diamond 2008a, 2008b, 2008c), even if it has been followed by a cautious revival since 2009 (Carothers 2009a, 2012).

Throughout this period of backlash, the democracy promotion community has continued to insist that in its essence democracy promotion is *not* about regime change. Two methods of 'defence' have been put forward: 1) There has been a general effort to distance democracy promotion aims and justifications from those put forward for regime change. Interventions for regime change and democracy promotion, it is argued, are distinct foreign policy instruments; and whether we consider the former a legitimate or an illegitimate instrument, we must recognize their distinct and non-mutually-dependent aims. Regime change, to remove a dangerous dictator for security reasons, is not in any direct or foundational sense tied to the wish to promote democracy, which is a wider aim. Democracy promotion, too, may follow intervention which may have as its aim regime change, but democracy promotion per se is not in its essence about regime change. 2) Democracy promoters have started to emphasize and reinforce the non-coercive methods of democracy promotion – including democracy conditionalities, democracy assistance and democracy support. Through the use of these 'soft' instruments it is assumed the connection between regime change – expected to take the form of military intervention – and democracy promotion can be severed.

What is interesting to note is that these arguments have failed to convince many. Not only do many critics in the West lapse into the tendency to conflate regime change and democracy promotion but also, and more significantly, in the Arab world, the US is still perceived very negatively because of its regime change policies during the Iraq War. As recent polls illustrate, the Arabs do not want to partake in US democracy promotion which is perceived as an intrusion in their domestic affairs, but rather favour US support in building capacity and creation of economic opportunities through investments. As Zogby argues, even if belief in democracy promotion may be in the process of being reinvigorated, it is far less the case for Arab recipients of such a policy:

> While many Americans still want to see ourselves as 'the shining city on the hill', we simply do not understand that is not how most Arabs see us. Two disastrous and bloody wars in Iraq and Afghanistan; the blind eye we have shown to Israeli violations of Palestinian rights and life; Guantanamo and the horrors of Abu Ghraib; torture, rendition, and 'black sites'; and the treatment of Arabs and Muslims in America all have taken a toll on our credibility as advocates for democracy and human rights. (Zogby 2012)

Crucially, democracy promotion, in the eyes of the Arab population is still closely associated with interference in domestic affairs and thus regime change.

How should we then understand the relationship between democracy promotion and regime change? What explains the continuing association of regime change with democracy promotion, even in the face of the continued arguments by democracy promoters against such connection? Is democracy promotion regime change?

This chapter seeks to provide an answer to this question from the critical perspective. First, we introduce the history of regime change and show how it has morphed with 'democratic' ideals so as to produce what could today be called 'democratic interventionism'. We identify some core literature on this democratic interventionism before we move on to tackle, in the context of the rise of this form of interventionism, the two key defensive moves made by the democracy promotion community to distance themselves from the accusations that democratic interventionism is leading to the equation of regime change and democracy promotion. We evaluate, first, the argument that democracy promotion and regime change are separate agendas, and find this defence faulty. We then examine the argument that democracy promotion today takes the form of consensual and non-coercive methods. We argue that the 'soft' methods of democracy promotion today can be seen as far less 'soft' and 'benign' than they appear at first sight. A sliding scale of coercion, with a preference for softer instruments at present, seems to characterize 'democratic interventionism' today. A critical theoretical perspective, we argue, allows us to fruitfully grapple with the difficult question 'Is democracy regime change?' and responds 'yes, so it would seem'.

From regime change to democratic interventionism?

Strategies of regime change can be traced back to the early Cold War period when in the American foreign policy circles, in the context of various critiques of Truman's doctrine of containment in relation to the USSR, some started calling for a more aggressive strategy against the Soviets. Such a strategy came to be known as 'rollback'. Regime change, or rollback, is a type of intervention that intends to alter the status quo of a country's governing regime and seeks to do so in an assertive way: 'Rollback strategies seek not merely to contain the target state within its borders but to overthrow its ruling regime through a variety of mechanisms, ranging from covert intelligence operations to overt support for an external opposition group' (Litwak 2007: 110). The aim is to facilitate a change of regime which favours the interests of the intervening state: regime change, traditionally, is not conducted for altruistic reasons but for ends which serve the intervening power's interests (security, economic) in one way or another.

The existing literature on regime change tends to emphasize the violent nature of such an intervention. Regime change is explained as relying on a significant degree of coercion to facilitate the accession of a 'better' regime which is to replace a discredited one: 'regime change – in its modern usage – [is] the forcible replacement by external actors of the elite and/or governance structure of a state so that the successor regime approximates some purported international standards of governance' (Reisman 2004: 516).

But what is the relationship between regime change and democracy promotion? This is an interesting question, for increasingly, interventions in other states are justified in terms of 'democratization' of a state. Indeed, if during the Cold War regime change was not regime-type specific, in the post-Cold War environment, the democratic nature of any new regime has been a key determining factor in assessment of the legitimacy of the intervention. It is almost inconceivable for key Western actors today to advocate regime change in favour of a non-democratic regime, despite the record of support to such regimes in the past.

As a result of this interesting morphing of democratic expectations and regime change, a growing body of literature in political science has started to study in more detail the rationales for, and the consequences of, the emerging paradigm of 'democratic interventionism'. Such a form of intervention seems to be in line with regime change in objectives (that is, protection of external power's economic and security interests) but overlaps with democracy promotion in identifying transition to democracy as a key underpinning objective of 'regime change'.

One influential group of studies that has sought to bring together study of democracy and security has been the so-called democratic peace literature. The democratic peace thesis argues that evidence shows that democracies rarely fight each other, which in turn explains efforts to democratize through intervention (Bueno de Mesquita 1999; Chan 1984; Lake 1992; Maoz and Abdolali 1989; Maoz and Russett 1993; Russett 1990; Weede 1984). Not all political scientists agree with the democratic peace thesis, however. For example, Mansfield and Snyder (1995, 2005) argue that democratization is a long and 'rocky' process, 'where mass politics mixes with authoritarian elite politics in a volatile way' (1995: 79; see also Vincent 1987; Layne 1994). They show that during a transition period, democratizing countries tend to be more aggressive and fight each other or other democracies. As a result, 'democratic interventionism' too should be considered with substantial scepticism, not just in its moral justifications but also the expected outcome of any intervention.

This literature has been helpful in trying to shed light on the (not-so-straightforward) consequences of democratization for stability. But this literature of course does not take a stance on the methods of intervention per se; democratic peace theorists are political scientists and do not advocate military forms of intervention (for an alternative view see Smith 2007; Ish-Shalom 2006).

Yet, others have tackled this aspect of democratic interventionism. Some argue that there is a direct correlation between military intervention and democratization (Meernik 1996; Hermann and Kegley 1998; Peceny 1999; Pickering and Peceny 2006). This suggests that military interventions, specifically, are apt in facilitating democratization. While some nuance this understanding of the results of democratic interventionism (Kegley and Hermann, 1997; Huntington, 1991; Muravchik, 1991; Forsythe, 1992; Coyne, 2008; Sullivan, 2008), overall, there is an agreement in the literature that the dividends of such a democratic aggressive expansionist policy can be desirable (Meernik 1996: 392).

This sort of an argument creates a problem for democracy promoters. This is because, with the increasing acceptance of democratic interventionism and its aligning with security and economic interests, the democracy promotion agenda starts to become morphed into discussions which originate with concerns about regime change. This is problematic because, in the minds of democracy promotion practitioners, this agenda did not arise from military interventionism, nor do many practitioners look kindly upon any such interventionism. Indeed, today most democracy promoters lament the bringing together of regime change thinking and democratic discourses. This is because the effect has been the gradual discrediting of democracy promotion. Notably, the close association of regime change and democracy promotion in Iraq and Afghanistan, they point out, has been a disastrous development for democracy promotion work: these interventions have single-handedly resulted in the 'backlash' against democracy promotion (Carothers 2006) and the increased scepticism around the world of Western democracy promotion policies (Whitehead 2009).

As a result, democracy promotion practitioners have developed responses to such critiques. But how viable are these responses to accusations that democracy promotion is just another phrase for regime change? We argue below that the efforts to distance democracy promotion and regime change in terms of both their *aims* and their *means* fail to convince. This is because, from a critical perspective, we are forced to observe the contradictions inherent in such responses. We argue that all forms of democracy promotion, from the coercive to the consensual, are suggestive of regime change.

Responding to democratic interventionism: distancing the agendas

Iraq and Afghanistan created real problems for democracy promoters. While the pro-democracy agenda had been 'on the roll' since the 1990s and had on the whole been welcomed around the world amongst democratizing communities, these interventions (justified in the first instance by security rationales but later attached to the notion of democracy promotion) created an immediate and long-lasting backlash against promotion of democracy. It is in response to these cases then that democracy promoters have sought, in the last ten years or so, through various rhetorical and argumentative as well as practical means, to distance themselves from any advocates of regime change.

The first response has been to emphasize in general terms the essential differences between the aims and justifications of regime change as opposed to democracy promotion. Promotion of war in defence of democracy, many democracy promoters argue, is actually perverse and a difficult foreign policy position to maintain. It is also a policy, which in the long-term can undermine the credibility of democratic countries' foreign policy.

With this in mind, it is no surprise that democracy promoters would emphasis that, while there may be legitimate interests to engage in regime change, this policy should be undertaken, and conceived of, as essentially separate from any attempt to democratize a state. Legitimate reasons may indeed exist for regime change – for example, the instability caused by proliferation of WMD and the potential transfer of these weapons to terrorist groups – but these are essentially separate from any attempt to democratize a state (a process which may unfold in the aftermath of an intervention attempting to remove a dangerous regime and the aim of which is to institute just and stable social relations between individuals and state institutions). The necessity to replace regimes that could potentially collaborate and arm terrorist organizations thus constitute potentially valid justifications for regime change, but the picture should not be confused with the democracy agenda itself, which is motivated by values of liberty, justice and rights.

However, from the critical perspective, we must observe the inherent problems with such a defensive distancing of these agendas. First, the close intertwining of democracy as an end value and the interests of actors in stability and security arguably make it very difficult for a plausible separation between the agendas to be made. How could we, for example, plausibly separate security interests and democracy as end values in Iraq? Regime change was seen as the only option as relationships with tyrannical regimes, such as Saddam Hussein's, were seen as difficult to sustain because 'American interests and those of tyrannical regimes inevitably clash' (Kagan and Kristol 2004: 68). This clash is based on an opposition between a US-supported international order extolling values of political and economic freedom, and anti-liberal ideologies presented by tyrannical regimes (Bridoux 2011a: 80–1). Not satisfied with the global promotion of US ideals through influence, G.W. Bush wanted 'the eradication of hostile regimes through means ranging from economic and diplomatic sanctions to military interventions, and their replacement with regimes more in line with US interests and less threatening to America and world security' (Bridoux 2011a: 80).

Today, it is arguably the very authoritarian nature of regimes (rather than their threatening actions or language per se) that is identified as problematic and the solution to the problem becomes to implement *democratic* regime change. This inherently ties democracy to regime change. In a sense, one could argue that democracy promoters have been *too successful* for their own good in promulgating and promoting the language and justifications of democratic governance. So mainstreamed is now democracy as a criteria of modern civilized governance that even violent policies, which most democracy promoters would abhor, become interpreted in terms of a democratic set of expectations.

Importantly, the critical approach identified here forces us to reflect on the intertwining of ideology, language, interests and power in democracy promotion and regime change. It could be argued that the very idea of democratic interventionism shows that the ideology of democracy has become firmly embedded in foreign policy discourses of a more 'realist' or 'instrumental' kind. As a result, crucially, dismembering the argumentative logics – even by democracy promoters – becomes difficult. They are captured in a rhetorical and linguistic trap. Whether or not democracy should entail regime change, it becomes impossible for democracy promoters to plausibly disengage from a discourse of democratic interventionism which brings together value promotion of democracy and security promotion through democratic criteria.

But what about the other defensive strategy? What about the claim that democracy promotion today has nothing to do with regime change because the methods and tools are inherently peaceful and consensual?

Democracy promotion as 'soft' tool of 'support'

The first defence against association of democracy promotion and regime change relies on an emphasis on the differential aims and justifications for the (presumably) different types of policy. But another defence relies on emphasis on different types of methods. So far we have associated regime change with violent and coercive intervention. This could be called the 'imposition' of a democratic regime (see Box 4.1 for case study). In the case of imposition of a democratic regime, the intervening power deploys overt and/or covert use of force that targets the government of the state under attack. The most recent and obvious examples of an imposed democratic regime could be said to be the invasions of Afghanistan and Iraq by a coalition led by the United States.

But such an assertive policy that aims at destabilizing a regime through open war can backfire and lead public opinion at home and abroad to question the actors involved. And it is this method of 'regime change' specifically that many democracy promoters take exception to.

Box 4.1 Democracy by imposition: The Iraq War of 2003

The invasion of Iraq by a coalition led by the United States in 2003, but perhaps more specifically, the subsequent occupation and reconstruction of Iraq, could be analysed as a case of coercive democratic intervention. Interestingly, in the months leading to the intervention, the promotion of democracy through regime change in Iraq was not explicitly part of the justificatory rhetoric of the G.W. Bush administration. Indeed, the justification for war relied mainly on a mix of security interests and normative stances regarding the nature of Saddam Hussein's regime. More specifically, there was a strong belief across the US administration that Saddam Hussein's regime, because it was autocratic, constituted a threat to regional and global instability. This potential instability would then take the form of weapons of mass destruction proliferation, magnified by alleged links Hussein's regime had with international terrorism (Bush 2000: 27; Boot 2004: 49). Indeed, in his 'Axis of Evil' speech, Bush identifies Iraq, Iran and Syria as rogue states and potential targets for regime change (Bush 2002). In the wake of the 9/11 attacks on the United States, such a discourse resonated powerfully with the American public opinion, in search of answers to 9/11 and, perhaps more so, in search of culprits for the first attack on American soil since Pearl Harbor in 1941. The Bush doctrine enunciated in the US National Security Strategy 2002 is unequivocal as to the remedy to deal with such threats: regime change is to be implemented thanks to US military superiority, which allows for unilateral and pre-emptive actions. Not satisfied with the mere global promotion of American ideals and principles through influence, G.W. Bush thus calls for the eradication of rogue regimes, through means ranging from economic and diplomatic sanctions to military intervention, and their replacement with democratic regimes more in line with US interests and less threatening to world security (Kagan and Kristol 1996: 7; Bridoux 2011: 80). However, it is interesting to note that the axis of evil identified by the US administration conveniently leaves aside friendly regimes that are anything but democratic. G.W. Bush and neoconservatives brushed aside these accusations and qualified these collaborations with undemocratic regimes against terrorist activities, as 'tactical deviations from a broad strategy of promoting liberal democratic governance throughout the world', resulting from direct threats to US security or from the absence of a viable democratic alternative (Kagan and Kristol 2000: 17). The difficulty to reconcile democracy promotion and use of force is encapsulated by a leading neoconservative, Charles Krauthammer (2004a, 2004b), who differentiates between Democratic Globalism and Democratic Realism. The latter lauds the suppression of the most threatening regimes first, while other dictatorships should be left alone and spared for the time being. Such a differentiation explains that the US can dispose of a Saddam while supporting Pakistan, frown at Syria and Iran and leave Communist China and North Korea literally unharmed. Democratic Realism thus merges traditional security considerations with a value-based policy of promoting democracy, through the use of force if need be. In the case of Iraq, it is because Saddam Hussein's regime was not democratic that security threats to the US and its allies became a clear and present danger that needed attention. The use of violence to remove Saddam from power and build a new democratic Iraq constitutes an extreme example of democratic intervention, which, as we witnessed once the regime was toppled, did not deliver, unable to deal with the loss of legitimacy caused by the use of violence in pursuit of democratic progress. Moreover, democracy promotion overall, in spite of its more peaceful expressions, was discredited and rejected in the US and more broadly as an expression of Western imperialism.

Not surprisingly democracy promoters have emphasized since the Iraq War that democracy promotion should not be understood as intertwined with such coercive instruments of change. They point out that arguably the tools most states and international organizations use today to promote democracy are explicitly non-coercive in nature – all the more so since the Iraq intervention. Today, various tools for enhancing democracy are put forward, from sanctions and conditionality policies to democracy assistance and civil society support, but none of these tools are coercive in nature – understood as relying on the use of force – and thus surely do not for this reason fit in with the 'coercive' idea of regime change tied up with the methods of military intervention.

This second line of defence against association of regime change and democracy promotion is seemingly plausible. Yet, analysis of different forms of more benign democratic intervention from a critical perspective reveals that even amongst the 'soft' tools of democracy enhancement lie dynamics which are suggestive of 'democratic interventionism' of a kind not a million miles removed from the aims and justifications of 'regime change'. We argue that even the softer forms of democracy promotion amount to what could be called 'democratic regime change'. The critical approach reveals power at work in the mechanisms of consensual methods of democracy promotion.

To explain how coercion and consent 'mix' in democracy promotion policies of various kinds, below we discuss in turn a range of 'soft' methods of democracy promotion. We start from analysis of power in the use of sanctions and condition-alities and move eventually towards the seemingly purely consensual mechanisms of civil society aid and democracy support. A sliding scale of power projection can be observed and as such a sliding scale of 'democratic interventionism' emerges from the study.

Pressured democratic regime change: The use of sanctions and threats

'Pressured democratic regime change' involves typically an intervention that entails putting pressure on a non-democratic government to liberalize its political regime and civil society. In so doing various sanctions and conditionality arrangements can be put in place to make it difficult for a state to continue to conduct its affairs in a non-democratic manner. The intervening power can also support non-state groups, typically exiled or home-based clandestine opposition groups, and may overtly or covertly finance their efforts to destabilize the regime. The intervening power can also, and usually will, try to secure the support of international or regional organi-zations to provide international legitimacy to this set of actions. Indeed, the intervening power tends to associate two types of instruments in its quest to generate regime change: a) material pressure through the use of economic and military sanctions, and the threat of the use of force; and b) moral influence by calling the international community to support its actions, in an effort to isolate the target regime. This is a type of intervention that largely privileges overt means of constraint.

Amongst sanctions or use of threats to generate political change, economic sanctions have been widely applied in the post-Second World War period and the post-Cold War era and remain the usual first weapon of choice for interveners. Elliott defines economic sanctions as involving 'reducing or even eliminating the flow of goods and/or money between a *sender* country, the country imposing sanctions, and a *target* country' (Elliott 1992: 97).

Box 4.2 Sanctioning Iraq 1991

A typical case of economic sanctions is Iraq in the 1990s. After the invasion and occupation of Kuwait by Saddam Hussein, the United Nations passed Resolution 661 that placed sanctions on the Iraqi regime to 'restore the authority of the legitimate government of Kuwait' (UNSC 1990). The resolution calls all states to suspend all imports of goods from Iraq and Kuwait; all activities by their nationals that facilitate the export of any commodities or products from Iraq and Kuwait; the export of any goods (especially military equipment) except medical supplies and, in humanitarian circumstances, foodstuffs to Iraq and Kuwait or their representatives. The international community, to punish Iraq for the invasion of Kuwait and her refusal to leave the country, thus implemented this set of economic and financial sanctions. Faced with Saddam Hussein's refusal to abide by requests to withdraw, the United Nations then allowed a coalition led by the United States to liberate Kuwait. Interestingly, the sanctions regime remained in place after this objective was achieved. Indeed, under US leadership, the UN then maintained the existing sanctions against Iraq with the purpose of disarming Saddam Hussein of his ballistic missiles, and chemical and biological weapons stockpiles (UNSC 1991a) to limit the threat posed by his regime to the regional stability. Finally, the reprisals launched by Saddam Hussein against the Kurds and Shias, who had been supportive of the coalition's invasion of Iraq, triggered yet another UNSC resolution calling for the Iraqi regime to stop the repression of the Iraqi population (UNSC 1991b). It is the combination of Saddam Hussein's reluctance to facilitate the work of disarmament inspectors, the repression of his political opponents, and the fact that his regime constituted a permanent threat to regional security, which drove the US to lead the charge in favour of regime change in Iraq. The first expression of this strategy was a statement by George H. Bush on 20 May 1991 insisting that the US will not lift sanctions as long as Saddam Hussein is in power. The US was thus determined 'to drive Mr. Hussein from power through a postwar policy of economic strangulation' (Tyler 1991). It is interesting to note that, in this case, the rationale and purpose of economic sanctions moved from punishment of deliberate aggression of one state against another to a deliberate attempt at generating regime change indigenously without further military intervention on behalf of the international community.

Pressured regime change underlines the fact that often it is useful to mix hard and more consensual power instruments in one's strategy of regime change. Pressured regime change does not involve use of military force but at the same time it hardly hides the fact that the use of sanctions or threats is above all a coercive mechanism of power. Indeed, should the target state of pressure refuse to give in, military intervention is almost always likely to follow. Pressured democratic regime then shows that 'interventionist' strategies for regime change inevitably blur military coercion and softer forms of pressure. Indeed, in some cases it can be hard to identify where coercion stops and consent starts. In this context, then, it is important to note that 'regime change' could be seen to be the aim of 'pressurizing' a state through a sanctions regime.

Even if we were right to say that this form of democracy promotion may in certain respects morph with regime change, surely this is not the case, however, with other activities of democracy promoters. Even if to put the pressure on regimes to get them to democratize may come to resemble a type of regime change, critics would argue that this form of action is rare in democracy promotion as much of the activity of democracy promotion today involves aid and other forms of consensual support to democratizing states and actors. Surely here coercive power cannot be identified, and we must accept that 'regime change' is not a very valid category of thought.

Aid conditionality

There are (at least) two strategies of democratic interventionism that are explicitly 'benign', cooperative and rely on consent-generation within and amongst target governments, civil society actors and populations with regard to the process of political and economic liberalization.

One key mechanism of democracy promotion has become development aid to recipient countries. This aid comes in various forms. Thus, first, various budget-lines of democratizing states today are supported directly by Western democracy instruments in order to encourage democratic reforms in bureaucratic service or military structures. The money in budget support is received in exchange for proof of active improvements in democratic life in target states – whether it is in terms of improved accountability of civil service decision-making, tackling of governmental corruption or improved public service delivery. While obtaining the proof of improvements made has been difficult, the donors and the recipients prefer these 'aid at a distance' instruments, partly because they demonstrate that today democracy aid can be delivered in a manner which is in line with the principle of 'local ownership'. While accountable to Western donors, it is the target state administrations that design, deliver, monitor and report on the use of western budget support funds.

Other types of 'democracy aid conditionalities' are also available. Thus, democracy promoters can – as the EU discovered – offer conditionality arrangements in inventive forms. For example, the carrot of offering membership in Western alliances or organizations can be an extremely productive democratizing force for states (Schimmelfennig and Scholtz 2008). Instead of granting full membership, more limited carrots are offered: for example, access to Western markets or other forms of co-operative arrangements as applied in European Partnership Agreements. Also, economic aid can become conditioned by what donors consider progress in the political and economic liberalization of a target country. Whatever the carrot – trade concessions, market access or direct budget support – the principle of this form of democracy promotion is that Western democracy donors seek to put in place 'conditions' which provide a gentle push for democratizing countries to implement democratic reforms.

What is important to note is that such a process of democratic aid conditioning is clearly driven by donor-states, which are in the position to specify the 'roadmap' to liberalization that has to be accepted and implemented by the government of the recipient country. It is donors' requirements with regard to liberalization that set the scene for the exchanges. This means that power relations are far from unequal, then, in these arrangements: the donors push the recipients to governance adjustments. Regimes are changed in exchange for money or other goods which developing countries often are dependent or become dependent on, and democratic requirements made inevitably thrusts recipient countries towards adoption of specific sets of reforms which tend to liberalize both economic and political realms – even if 'democratic' credentials of these forms of reform are not always appreciated 'locally' (Abrahamsen 2000). Through aid conditionality potential recipients of aid can then be compelled to adopt reforms and thus, curiously, become their own 'managers' in delivering for the donors (Abrahamsen 2004).

Hence, democratic aid conditionality as a strategy of democratic interventionism, it can be argued, is both a consent-based approach but also impositional in its own ways. Donors have an array of instruments that organize the de facto submission of recipients to their will. The relationship between donors and recipient governments is essentially a hierarchical relationship. It is also often a relationship which reflects structural dependency as it is embedded in contracts with obligations on behalf of the recipients of aid to perform in order to benefit from economic aid.

Thus, while falling short of actual use of force, it could be argued that in fact democratic aid conditionality of this kind is actually rather an intrusive mechanism, and in fact suggestive of 'democratic interventionism' that implicitly drives whole societies and state apparatuses in the direction of political and economic liberalization, essentially on donors' terms. In this sense it could be said to be about 'regime change', in accordance with donors' conceptions of what a good regime looks like.

But even if this was to be accepted, what about the softer forms of democracy promotion, often today referred to through the ideas of democracy assistance or democracy support?

Democracy assistance and democracy support?

Following the unwelcome association of democracy promotion with regime change through the use of force, a segment of the US academic and policy-making communities called for a change of policy regarding the promotion of democracy by US agencies (Lennon 2009). Instead of practicing democracy promotion, which is perceived as an imposition of a Western model of democracy on target countries, usually through a rather assertive backing of pro-democratic groups in third countries by US and other Western democracy promotion actors, 'democracy support' took over as a generic term to describe the activities of those actors. This form of support is closely tied with the already long-existing strategy of achieving democratic change through 'democracy assistance' from the ground up (Lennon 2009).

Box 4.3 Conditionality and MCC

The Millennium Challenge Corporation (MCC) illustrates the use of economic aid conditionality to push through a democratic agenda. The MCC is an independent foreign aid agency created by the US Congress in 2004 with the aim to fight global poverty. The agency delivers bilateral aid to the world's poorest countries, but only to those committed to good governance, economic freedom, and investment in their citizens. In contrast to more traditional donors, the MCC's criteria of eligibility for aid has democracy at its centre, which stems from the belief that development relies on economic growth and democracy: 'strong democratic institutions are some of the very institutions which enable sustainable, locally owned, positive economic outcomes' (MCC 2007: ii). Thus, MCC's aid compacts[1] are conditioned by the acceptance of the recipients of aid to trigger or deepen the political and economic liberalization of their societies: 'MCC's selection process incentivizes democratic transition by recognizing and providing resources for poverty reduction and economic growth programs to governments that demonstrate true commitment to democracy' (ii).

Once political and economic liberalization is on the move, partner countries are then asked to implement an accountability and transparency mechanism that actively involves the civil society and the private sector. MCC recommends an active participation of representatives of CSOs and the private sector in advisory boards that oversee the implementation of the compact, and the securing of the population's access to information or civic participation in government (MCC 2011: 1–2).

In democratic aid conditionality, the political and economic dimensions of liberalization are unsurprisingly closely linked. Both liberal democracy and free markets are identified as the best means to achieve economic growth and hence development. Actually, democratic institutions are considered as facilitators of the operations of a free market economy. The political content of MCC compacts focuses on just and democratic governance to promote political pluralism, equality and the rule of law; the respect of human and civil rights; the protection of private property rights; the encouragement of transparency and accountability of governments; and the fight against corruption. These values and institutions are representative of a neoliberal democratic conception of democracy. Indeed, the MCC encourages its partner countries to develop policies that lead firms and citizens to embrace and support global trade and international capital markets, to promote private sector growth, to strengthen market forces in the economy, and to respect workers' rights including the right to form labour unions for the sake of social stability, conducive to smooth operations of a market economy (MCC 2011: 5–6).

Yet, it is interesting to note that the MCC strongly supports the involvement of stakeholders (government, private sector and citizens) in the definition and the supervision of the implementation of aid compacts, as well as civic participation in government. This willingness to promote citizen empowerment and their active participation in public decision-making, however, are only light touches of a truly comprehensive expression of participatory democracy. Instead, the end goal of this involvement of non-governmental actors occurs merely in the name of accountability and transparency of governmental actions, effective functioning of societal institutions, and defusing of social tensions generated by inequalities caused by the functioning of a capitalist economy. According to MCC's logic, free markets need social order as well as little interference from the state to function effectively, and generate economic growth and thus development.

Assisting and supporting democracy involves a more 'modest, realistic and incremental approach' to democratic change that privileges the idea of partnership between donors and recipients of democracy aid (Diamond 2009: 33). Democracy assistance and support, the argument goes, is thus multilateral and collaborative and is responsive to target countries' initiatives and demands. It seeks to bypass the accusations of double standards – donors pushing for democracy in some regions/countries but not in others where they have security and economic interests; democracy support, while acknowledging the importance of other strategic interests, seeks to peacefully engage autocratic regimes and especially their societies (Lennon 2009: v; Carothers 2012).

Democracy support relies essentially on democracy assistance to achieve its objectives. Democracy assistance is the ensemble of techniques and instruments that are activated to implement democracy support programmes. Democracy assistance thus includes programming, sourcing of partners, technical support of target governments and NGOs – training, financial and material support, follow up, and assessment of programmes' effectiveness. For example, the US administration develops democracy assistance programmes around four pillars: civil society, elections and political processes, governance, and rule of law. US governmental democracy support actors then rely on a sophisticated procurement system *to choose organizations they will work with* – both US-based NGOs and the target country's NGOs. Those NGOs are in charge of deploying an array of techniques to achieve the aims specified in the programmes that are implemented. Achievements are constantly monitored according to specific assessment methods to ensure that the programmes financed by the US government progress according to plan.

But what does democracy support actually mean in practice? Ownership and empowerment of target countries – governments and civil societies – are the two concepts at the core of the idea of 'supporting' democracy. Descriptions of democracy support in action never fail to emphasize how the 'locals' are in charge of the design and implementation of democratization programmes. For example, the US support of the Namibian transition to democracy illustrates the meaning of democracy support. The US government, through the United States Agency for International Development (USAID), responded to a request of the Namibian government and the legislature to support the country's transition. USAID has provided technical assistance to the Namibian Parliament and supported Namibian civil society since 1995. Programmes offer technical training on democratic procedures and principles in the parliament, and technical and financial assistance to civil society groups to organize their communication with the government and parliament. This support also translated into the foundation of the Namibian Democracy Support Centre, 'an autonomous organization that is dedicated to strengthening the interaction between Parliament, other government institutions, and civil society in a planned manner' (Barr 2005). We find here a similar emphasis on a central dimension of democracy support: participation and empowerment of the government and civil society of target countries. The rationale of democracy support consists in broadening the range of actors as well as their access to the political game, as Barr concludes: 'We are encouraged by the possibility of greater collaboration between the United States and Namibia on behalf of the social, political, and economic empowerment of Namibians' (Barr 2005). In the case of Namibia, it appears that USAID was thus more responsive than assertive in its support to the country's government and civil society.

Another more recent example of democracy support is the Tunisian transition to democracy that followed the January 2011 uprising against President Ben Ali's regime. When asked about the electoral process, a USAID Democracy Officer explained that Tunisians were in charge of the process from the start:

> Tunisians were very clear that they would lead the transition, that they have a vision, and that they would manage this process based on priorities expressed by Tunisian citizens. USAID contributed to this process by supporting peer-to-peer networking opportunities between Tunisian reformers and those from other parts of the world, based on Tunisian requests. Through those peer-to-peer consultations, democratic reformers shared best practices regarding transparent election processes, systems, and grass roots political campaigning. (USAID 2012: 10–11)

The USAID Democracy Officer then emphasized that the Tunisian experience sends a clear message across the Middle East, but also to donors. The Tunisian uprising shows that, while an inspiration, uprisings in another Middle Eastern and North African countries have their own characteristics, 'their own unique character and will follow different trajectories' (USAID 2012: 11). The job of USAID is to *support* these transitions so that they meet the expectations of citizens, not of any external power. Democracy support is thus presented as a rather passive interventionist strategy. It is reactive to requests from recipient countries and its content is the fruit of close partnership and collaboration between donor and recipient countries.

But is democracy support as neutral as it seems? And is democracy support beyond the scope of accusations that democracy promotion equals 'regime change'? We argue that it is not. This is because multiple power relations are at work in democracy support too, and at the same time the sliding scale of democratic interventionism continues to loom large in the background of democracy support.

But how do power relations come through in democracy support? As has been emphasized in Chapters 3 and 5, donors remain free *to choose organizations they will work with*. And who are these organizations? They are essentially organizations and populations that are marginalized within their own societies. Indeed, most democracy promoters help indigenous people, tribal groups, women, etc. Yet, in addition to such a positive bias, democracy promoters also tend, in the words of a senior UN official, 'to fund people like us, we tend to be impressed with people who can use our discourse, people who can somehow plug into the way we like to think about the way the world looks' (Chatham House, 2012). By supporting the liberal activists that come forward for support, donors do manage to support democratic forces. Yet, in so doing they also actively support forces in favour of those kinds of activities which they see as central for liberal democratization. Liberals who think and act like donors will be offered the capacity to function, and hence to push for political and economic liberalization in their countries. Other actors, even though democratic but more often than not anti-American or anti-European and often anti-liberal, tend not to benefit from democracy assistance (Crawford and Abdulai 2012; Ayers 2006; Abrahamsen 2000; Kurki 2011; Bridoux 2011b). Consequently, it is not 'their' regime that will emerge, but the regime promoted by liberal local actors of democratization, as designed and supported by Western donors.

Box 4.4 Conditioning Civil Society in Ghana

The Ghana Research and Advocacy Programme (G-RAP) and the Ghana Rights and Voice Initiative (RAVI) are two civil society development programmes implemented in Ghana between 2006 and 2010. Both programmes are funded by international donors (the Netherlands, United Kingdom, Denmark and Canada fund G-RAP, while RAVI is funded by the United Kingdom). The rationale of both programmes consists in the reinforcement of civil society's capacity to hold the Ghanaian government accountable for its actions within the context of the Ghana Poverty Reduction Strategy entrusted to the government of Ghana by international aid donors. Consequently, G-RAP and RAVI support pro-poor and pro-equality civil society organizations that work for a more transparent, accountable and responsive government, especially towards its poorest citizens.

In selecting civil society organizations to benefit from their funding, G-RAP and RAVI privilege organizations that have displayed an ability to engage and hold the government of Ghana to account for its actions. Crawford and Abdulai argue that both programmes deliberately set selection criteria that privilege specific Research and Advocacy Organizations already established in government circles instead of community-based organizations, which would then have offered support to broad-based civil society in Ghana. Indeed, these selection criteria included: 'the demonstration of existing capacity through satisfactory responses in a highly demanding organizational assessment of 109 questions; an emphasis on both research and advocacy activities; and above all, an annual financial turnover of at least US$400,000' (Crawford and Abdulai 2012: 136–7). Hence, smaller organizations were de facto pushed away from applications. Instead, organizations already funded by donors, organizations that tend to be typically pro-market and liberal oriented received the bulk of financial support. Indeed, eight out of nine organizations funded under the G-RAP programme openly declare to work to promote democracy, good governance and an open economic environment in Ghana. Only one funded organization, the Third World Network, focuses on socio-economic development issues and especially social justice, and can be described as 'a persistent critic of the neo-liberal development strategies promoted by donor agencies' (Crawford and Abdulai 2012: 137).

Thus, the research by Crawford and Abdulai suggests that the RAVI programme, and perhaps more so the G-RAP programme, organize their financial support on the basis of a specific ideological commitment to turn the Ghanaian civil society into a mechanism to control the activities of the state. The Ghanaian government is thus identified by donors as untrustworthy, probably unwilling and unable to actually 'implement donors' preferred policy choices, ones that remain economically neo-liberal while being labeled pro-poor' (Crawford and Abdulai 2012: 147). Not only is the civil society in Ghana rebuilt on a Western model of active liberal watchdog civil society, but it appears that to precisely reformat civil society on such a model allows donor countries to go around an issue they created: the transition from highly directive structural adjustment programmes and conditionality to less directive poverty reduction strategies that have the notion of country ownership at heart. Such a transition caused a reduction in control by aid donors over recipient countries. Thus, as in the case of Ghana, to make use of civil society as a mechanism to counter and control the power of the Ghanaian state allows donors to still exercise direction over the government of Ghana by proxy: a selected elite of NGOs that have the capacity to engage effectively with their government play a transmission role of donors' influence on Ghana's policies to make sure that 'government policies remain consistent with their own policy choices, that is, ones that promote economic liberalization and private sector development' (Crawford and Abdulai 2012: 149).

Therefore, we argue that the shift from democracy promotion to democracy support is actually confined to rhetoric. In practice, Western donors still promote a very specific form of democracy and expect little contestation from recipients regarding its deployment. As a result a hegemony of ideas and the power relations attached to it (discussed in more detail in Chapter 7) tends to flow from the donors to the recipients. As far as more 'benign' forms of democratic interventionism are concerned, we find that they may not be as 'pluralistic', 'local' and 'benign' as they are often made out to be but are also embedded in relations and strategies of power and have power-effects in target countries, which may be empowering for liberal actors but disempowering for other types of democratic actors.

Conclusion

On the odd occasion – perhaps most notably in Iraq and Afghanistan – democracy promotion and regime change foreign policies became visibly aligned. Ever since then democracy promoters have been concerned about the alignment of these two concepts in world politics and have sought to fight it through various conceptual and practical arguments. Yet, we have argued here that there are no easy answers to the alignment of these agendas. This is because it may be that democracy promotion is, even when not practiced as in Iraq or Afghanistan, a form of regime change; in other words, from a critical perspective, the sliding scale between military intervention and benign consensual forms of democracy promotion may be somewhat more slippery than it is often assumed.

While soft instruments of change are increasingly used, the objective of promoting freedom and democracy becomes surprisingly 'coercive' and 'forceful' when the means of such propagation are under close scrutiny. From military intervention and sanctions to conditionality and democracy support, power relations and hierarchies are embedded in democracy promotion. This is probably why many critics and recipients remain sceptical of democracy promotion. Even the so-called soft power instruments are instruments of power. The unmatched position of power in the international system of democracy promoters feeds into the policy agenda and its instruments.

So, does democracy promotion systematically mean regime change? From the perspective of officials and practitioners active in this field, democracy promotion does not mean regime change, and never did. Democracy promotion is not about invading countries with all guns blazing, or about wilfully toppling authoritarian regimes. Democracy promotion, for them, is about patient supportive nurturing of players in authoritarian and semi-democratic countries, which will, eventually, help to generate the conditions needed for a peaceful democratic transition to take place. However, from the critical perspective, and from the perspectives of some of the targets of democracy promotion, such a benign understanding of democracy promotion policies is not so obvious. Democracy promotion, we have shown here, seems to *always* involve a certain degree of intervention and mingling in domestic affairs of states. That is, even when softer tools of democracy promotion are used; it seems that a particular type of intervention – a democratic intervention of a consensual kind – is envisaged. In this sense, even as military intervention is rejected today, there seems to be still a hidden convergence between democracy promotion and support and 'regime change'.

As Chapter 5 will explore, this omnipresence of Western power in defining what and how democracy is promoted inevitably generates questions about the context-sensitive nature of democracy promotion, even though its supporters argue that today, democracy promotion is all about the 'local'.

Notes

1. Thus leading some authors to label the US a rogue state itself because of the inevitable instability such a policy would generate. See McClintock (1992); Chomsky and Herman (1979); George (1991); Joes (1999, esp. 93–125); Caraley (1999); Martinot (2003); Prestowitz (2003).
2. A Compact is a multi-year agreement between the Millennium Challenge Corporation and an eligible country to fund specific programmes targeted at reducing poverty and stimulating economic growth (MCC 2013).

5 Is democracy promotion context-sensitive?

The advocates of democracy promotion often perceive the universal promotion of human rights and democracy as a self-evidently progressive, unquestionably good and uncontested practice. Thus, the claim is that not only is democracy a universal value (Sen 1999), but democracy promotion is too (McFaul 2004–05). Yet this has not been uncritically accepted by all. As we have seen, many critics argue that the promotion of democracy is an imposition of Western governments on developing and weak states. Critics argue that not only does it benefit the interests of Western democratic states (see Chapter 3), but also, importantly, the developing states themselves have little say over what is promoted in their country. This is why Asian values or African values do not appear to be appreciated in democracy promotion: it is based, these critics argue, on the advancement of specific models and ideals conceived in the West on the rest of the world, with little interest in consideration of contextuality of values and practices of democracy or governance more generally.

But how persuasive are such criticisms today? Is democracy promotion really 'imposed' and non-context sensitive? How *do* democracy promoters today seek to take account of contestation over values and, crucially, the significance of the 'local' as a context where democracy aid 'lands'? How is the paradoxical relationship between 'promoting' an idea and recognizing democracy's local permutations squared in democracy promotion? And what does a critical approach contribute to analysis of such questions?

It is significant to note that democracy promoters have in recent years sought explicitly to address the accusation that they do not provide 'context-sensitive' democracy assistance. Indeed, the very language of assistance and democracy support today reflects the moves made by democracy promoters to 'ground-up' forms of democratization, civil society support, participatory consultations and locally owned projects. But what do these moves mean, really, today? How context-sensitive and reflective of various possible paths of democratization is democracy promotion, assistance and support?

This chapter examines, first, the context for any discussions on context-sensitivity and how this issue was dealt with during the 1990s, considered as the 'golden age' of democracy promotion. It then examines the shifts towards more 'local' and 'sensitive' perspectives and what this means for democracy promotion. It is argued here that while shifts towards more localized perspectives have taken place and are significant in having changed the nature of democracy promotion, a critical theoretical perspective needs to interrogate in detailed terms the meaning and power relations of this 'localization'.

Arguably, when examined from a critical perspective, a 'pedagogy of power' – that is, a tendency of the powerful West to 'teach' the uneducated and powerless the ways of democratic modernisation (Teivainen 2009) – can still be observed at work in democracy support today, however 'localized' it is. Indeed, it is the new forms of power which emanate from attempts at localization and facilitation of country ownership which need to be paid careful attention to today, for they indicate changing forms of power relations in democracy promotion and perhaps in world politics more widely.

The 1990s – promotion of a universal ideal

The early 1990s saw many 'triumphalist' statements of the victory of Western values of liberal democracy and open markets. From Francis Fukuyama's (1989) famous 'end of history' thesis, to Plattner's (1993) or Mandelbaum's (2007) confidence in the 'universal value of democracy', the 1990s was a time for confident liberalism. It was a time when socialism and even social democratic alternatives were deemed to be passé, and liberalism had 'won the day'. The Eastern Europeans cried out for more liberal democracy and open markets and it is this demand that the democracy promoters sought to fill.

This was also the time of growth and expansion for the democracy industry. New actors – from the UN to the EU – came on to the scene and various NGOs – from Open Society Foundations to political foundations – strutted confidently to the ex-Soviet sphere and beyond in defence of the universal promise of more freedom through democracy and open markets.

Some significant breakthroughs were made in the 1990s in terms of global democratization. Thus, Eastern and Central Europe, for example, were pretty successfully brought into the fold of liberal democracy. Yet, backlashes and failures of democratization also followed. Despite the initial successes in Eastern Europe and in state-building contexts, there were also persistent problems in facilitation of democracy. Hybrid regimes and partial democratizations seemed to follow in many countries where democracy was funded. The role of international actors was not self-evidently positive, nor significant (Whitehead 1996; Pridham 2005). Importantly, some actors noted the increasing arguments regarding the 'inappropriateness' of Western engagement: for example, some argued that 'Asian values' were such that they made redundant or contextually problematic Western liberal ideals in non-Western contexts. Others noted that conditionality and occasionally even interventionist democracy promotion was too pushy and was perceived locally as colonialist, rather than universally acceptable.

While these concerns simmered away, the Iraq War brought to a head the backlash against democracy promotion. The association – false association in key regards (given that intervention was not made solely in the name of democracy) – of Iraq with 'democracy promotion' and the resulting failures of democratization in Iraq angered recipients of democracy aid around the world (see Carothers 2006). An agenda of American power projection could clearly be observed and the colonial or imperial overtones of American policy were revealed. With the increasing questioning of American and Western power, and the rise of new power centres, such as the BRICs, a new era of global power relations was perceived to be arising. Universalist, Western-centric, interventionist and unquestioningly liberal models of governance reform were called into question. Not only should 'the local' be considered and shaped for democratization to be successful, but so should the value systems of the locals, argue critics.

Shifts in language and practice

As has already been mentioned, a linguistic shift in democracy promotion took place in the early-mid-2000s and this language shift also reflected some real changes of direction in democracy support. As Carothers (1999) put it so well: there was indeed a 'learning curve' in action in democracy promotion. Let us set out some of the key shifts that this entailed.

One such key shift involved the development of democracy promotion language away from the idea or rhetoric of 'promotion'. In the context of Iraq and other failures of coercive democratization, it was deemed wise to speak instead of democracy assistance and support to democracy. The concept of assistance, as Burnell (2000) has argued, refers to the concrete practices of delivery of aid to democratizing forces – states or civil society actors – in target countries of democracy advocacy. The concept of democracy support is more complicated. It seems to lack clear definition, and is often used interchangeably with democracy promotion and assistance. As much as it has a distinct meaning, it seems to refer to the fact that democracy promoters today 'support' rather than 'impose' democracy in target countries. Promotion seems to now entail imposing and 'confident' pushing of Western values, whereas democracy activists and practitioners see democracy as 'locally engendered'. 'It cannot be exported but can be supported' is the new slogan in democracy circles today.

Hand in hand with this rhetorical shift goes a movement to the concept of 'local ownership'. This term, it could be argued, is not original to democracy circles, but rather evolved out of the debates about development prior to and during the Paris conference and declaration. The Paris Declaration of 2005 set out a new paradigm for development aid, and democracy assistance, as it is often tied to development aid, was conceived to fall under this declaration. What this declaration called for was more coordinated and cooperative aid processes and programmes, to avoid duplication and clashing of programmes, but also more 'locally owned' development programmes, projects and practices. Today, democracy promoters and supporters, from major states such as the US to the EU and UN, all recognize the need for 'local ownership' of democratization.

What does this mean in practice?

First, it means that democracy promotion should today be more about local projects and less about democracy promoters' visions. Thus, projects should now be locally 'demanded' or asked for by local state or civil society actors. Certainly, imposition through military intervention is shunned, and locally owned democratization is seen as the gold standard. This more locally owned vision can manifest itself through 'budget support' to state bureaucracies for reform, or civil society aid. In either case, both recipient states and civil society actors 'own' the projects.

Second, they do not just 'own them'; they also 'manage' them. Interestingly, there has been a shift towards increasing 'self-management' of democracy aid. While democracy promoters set out the criteria and management frameworks of democracy promotion projects, it is local state or civil society actors which implement and manage these projects, reporting finally to funders who then measure the 'effectiveness' of their actions.

This local ownership can manifest itself in facilitation of more 'incentive'-based democracy promotion programmes. Thus, sanctions and conditionalities of the hard kind have given way to the incentive structures of MCC or the EU neighbourhood policy (see Chapter 4). States and civil society actors, if they wish to reap the rewards of Western funding, should come to see themselves as benefiting from the incentives for further funding and aid set by the donors. It is 'up to them' to realize the rationality of democratization, helped with concrete carrots of development aid and investment offered as a reward.

Ownership has also manifested itself in increasing push for 'competition' as a tool of levelling the playing field between different actors competing for funding. Thus, civil society projects, for example, are today almost without exception funded through 'competition' for funds between different 'bidders' or 'applicants'. A market democracy – equal opportunity in applying for competitively distributed resources – rules in the allocation of funds to civil society actors.

Third, there has been a distinct move away from institutionally focused projects towards increasing interest in civil society aid. This in many ways arose from the problems of procedural democracy aid identified in the mid-1990s and the need to 'consolidate' (Diamond 1999) the workings of democracy in cultural shifts in the population. Indeed, it is not just state-pacts that now are sought but rather correct shifts in the mentalities of the people of the target countries. Democratization is not able to succeed unless 'the people' modernize and democratize their world views and come to embrace the vision of liberty and democracy as their future. This is why civil society funding and projects have been increasingly turned to as the 'hope' for democratization – often to the detriment of 'political institution' work, a fact pointed to today by many party political democracy promoters. This is arguably partly because working with 'depoliticized' civil society is less overtly political than classical institutional or party political support.

This is not all. Fourthly, shifts have also taken place from promotion of specific 'Western' values of liberty and democracy to 'partnerships' and 'dialogue'. No democracy promoter today dares suggest that Western values are promoted: instead, interestingly, most funders today recognize that there are 'multiple paths to democracy' and that 'democracy is a contested concept', the meaning of which needs to be explored 'locally'. They also call for partnership and participatory processes of democratization to be facilitated: consultations with people, dialogue with various actors and facilitation of 'stake-holder' engagement are seen as essential to democracy promotion, or support, today.

Given these shifts, it would seem as if a whole new paradigm of democracy promotion faces us. If so, and if the rhetoric of shifts is to be believed, certainly democracy promotion, or support, cannot today be perceived as 'imposed by the West'. What are, if any, the power relations in this form of locally owned democratization? We argue that they can only be accessed when attention is paid to the covert and implicit forms of power, rather than mere overt exercise of power. It is absolutely the case that more and more rarely today do donors exercise hard power to push democratizers to democratize – just reflect on the realities of Egyptian democratization. But does this mean that no power or influence is exerted through democracy support on target populations? No, the critical approach reveals subtle but important forms of power in these forms of 'local ownership', and indeed reveals that a 'pedagogy of power' still prevails even as the 'local ownership' paradigm reigns.

New forms of power

What forms of power can we, with the critical approach in mind, detect in the above four new dynamics of locally owned democratization? Let us examine them in turn.

First, the critical approach directs us to ask some questions of the kind of local ownership that is encouraged. When a state owns a reform process that the EU funds, to what extent is this process locally owned? The funders fear that the answer often is to too great an extent, because the accountability mechanisms are frequently poorly exercised and when projects finish it is 'too late' to challenge the use of the funds (for an interesting discussion of the pros and cons of budget support see European Commission 2008). At the same time, from a critical perspective one might argue that reform processes such as budget support are actually not particularly deeply locally owned. This is because the projects themselves are offered for particular types of reforms. Improving the efficiency of social services or fighting against corruption are important aspects of budget supported programmes. Are they locally owned? Only in name, many would argue, for in fact the aims and delivery methods, and measures of success and failure, are actually set by donors. This may in fact be the very reason for the failure of the projects.

What about local ownership of civil society projects? Surely these are locally owned? Surely it is the 'demand' in local contexts for democracy projects that donors seek to fulfil? This may not be the case. The practice suggests that in fact NGOs and civil society actors in local contexts often 'respond' to donor 'calls for proposals', rather than going to them to demand funds for their projects. Indeed, the entire calls for proposal system is designed in such a way as to facilitate the appearance of local ownership, while in fact funders remain in charge of the language, objectives, criteria and funding management structures of aid. As a result, NGOs either try to fit their agendas into the language and objectives of the donors or, in some instances, are even created in response to budget lines developed by funders. For example, examine the rise of civil society in the Arab Middle East in the aftermath of the Arab Spring: while for sure many NGOs and civil society movements arose in response to the liberalization of political realm, many more were established in response to the increased provision of funds for civil society actors.

Pedagogy of power (Teivainen 2009) is still at play essentially because donors prescribe the ways they engage with 'demand' for democracy. The donors offer what they perceive as important projects and programmes for democratization, which they presume the local actors will be interested in, or should be interested in. Does this mean that local ownership is achieved? It is doubtful, for in fact evidence suggests that local actors often rather pragmatically engage with donor agendas, while the meaning and uniqueness of their own aims remain a secondary point as they seek to show the funders their credentials and interests in liberal democracy promotion.

This is not all, however, for the problems of ownership do not just reside in interactions with those that are funded: key issues arise as to the extent to which democracy promoters 'see' political actors as legitimate in local country contexts at all. Indeed, it is striking that critics have consistently argued that mainly liberal and centre-ground actors receive extensive funding from democracy promoters and supporters, and that biases exist in who is funded (Ayers 2006; Lynch and Crawford 2011). Practitioners tend to deny this, arguing that all actors, from all political persuasions, are free to apply for funding. The problem here seems to be that some actors simply do not emerge as 'democratic' for many funders. Thus, in the EU system, anti-EU organizations, for example, are not expected to apply for funding: but of course being anti-European does not equate to being anti-democratic. The same applies to radical democratic actors in developing countries. Just because they are radical leftist actors arguing for non-open market systems, this does not mean they are necessarily anti-democratic, nor are necessarily Islamic activists. Their conceptions of democracy, and of the relationship between democracy and markets, simply differ sharply from those of the funders.

The inability to recognize this leaves deep imprints on 'locally owned' democracy promotion. Democracy is a subjective and value-laden concept and always interpreted from one perspective or another. This means that no 'neutral' apolitical perspective exists from which donors can evaluate what count as the most 'authentic' or 'locally' representative 'democratic' actors: they can only evaluate this from their perspective. When they do, they come to distort the meaning of democracy and democratic activism in target countries by funding often the kinds of actors they can 'recognize' as liberal democratic activists 'like themselves' (Chatham House 2012).

This is not problematic per se of course, but may be a problem reflective of democracy promotion as an inevitably biased practice. Yet, the current pretences of neutrality in engagement do not help to deal with this problem: the politics and the power consequences of democracy promotion 'horizons' need to be recognized.

What does this all mean for the practices of incentivization, market democracy and self-management in democracy promotion? It means that it may very well be the case that new forms of power are exerted through these new forms of 'locally owned' management of democracy promotion (Abrahamsen 2004; Kurki 2011). Incentivization, for example, may not be categorically very different from 'conditionality' because it is essentially based on the possibility to withhold financial resources if the recipient of development aid funds does not meet democratization criteria. The EU's new incentive structures – which claim to provide countries 'more for more' (more aid for more democratic reform) – sounds categorically different from sanctions or conditional responses. Yet, they may in fact be little more than a shift in a continuum of conditional perspectives. The fact of the matter remains, if a country wishes to maintain its aid relationship with the donors, they should show willingness to engage with the agendas and criteria for good governance set by the donors. How they engage with the agendas is for them to 'decide', but the agendas themselves are set in Washington and Brussels, and this is also where ability to meet the criteria for further funding and incentivization is 'measured'. Even if engagement with local stakeholders is built into the assessment, the knowledge and judgments produced are generated for the donors, often by the donors and according to donors' criteria, objectives and measures of success. Little room here exists for radical reconceptualization of the meaning of 'democracy' or 'success' of democratization from the 'local' perspective.

As for the market democracy system of civil society aid, we can see that this set of biases create some real problems in this system being able to deliver democracy aid equally for all. Even though all actors are equally able in principle to apply for funds, some are more equal than others in their ability to deliver 'for the donors' according to their wishes, objectives and criteria of management. Crucially, some are more willing than others to even consider applying for these funds. Indeed, radical democratic actors indicate that they do not wish to apply for EU or US funds because these funding streams would depoliticize and water down the radical democratic demands which these organizations wish to push for. Thus, they self-elect themselves out of the 'demand'-based system of support that the democracy promoters have set up. The consequences of this for the 'equality' and 'neutrality' of democracy support has to be considered. This is because, even as self-deselection is the cause of bias in democracy support, this bias can come to have important and deep-running consequences for the kinds of democracy which donors end up promoting and supporting. If only those actors which agree with the donors and their agendas are funded, only partial and potentially unstable and locally illegitimate forms of democratic government are created.

What of the self-management system which the donors have put into place? What is crucial to note about this principle that both states and civil societies should 'self-manage' their affairs in tune with the wishes, visions and demands of Western donors, is that it can be interpreted in line with the workings of a deeply power-ridden framework. As the critical approach highlights, power cannot be exercised successfully in the long-term through coercion and imposition; rather, consent of the citizens, willing engagement with the agendas of hegemons, is required for stability of a social order. Arguably, the idea of self-managed democracy promotion indicates the perfection of this system of 'democracy promotion' as 'self-governed' creation of a hegemonic social order. If activities of self-governed democratizers always have to and do (willingly) abide by the parameters set by the vision of the donors then surely it is hegemonic visions of society, economics and politics being created through these processes. The potential for contestation and power in societal interactions is being played down, while consensual agendas become 'self-evident' and 'embraced' by target populations of reform.

Box 5.1 Paradoxes of local ownership in Eastern European Neighbourhood Policy

One of the EU's key goals has been, through its Neighbourhood Policy, to encourage partnership relationships with countries on its eastern borders. The idea has been that fostering partnerships can facilitate processes of reform and cooperation. Yet, this has been a troubled process critics would argue. This is because, despite the language of cooperation and partnership, much of the inter-relationship is in fact premised on 'European' ideals, interests and ideas. On what basis are such claims made?

As critics of EU foreign policy have noted, there is a curious 'externalization' of governance tools and structures at the heart of EU external policy. Just as the accession or enlargement process entailed that countries which wished to join the Union should internalize the acquis communautaire[1] of the union, including all its legal and technical requirements for governance and market regulation, in the same sense the European Neighbourhood Policy, targeted at states which are outside of the expected 'accession sphere', seems to be premised on the assumption that cooperation and partnership is to be based on values, regulations and ideals set by Europe (Korosteleva 2011).

While there is formally a discussion and dialogue process attached to the negotiation of the so-called 'Action Plans' which guide the relationship between EU and Eastern neighbours, at the same time, critics argue that in fact little substantive dialogue takes place concerning the core substance of EU policy. Thus, it is European values that are the 'shared values', and it is EU priorities that are the shared cooperation priorities. It is also EU understandings of a modern state which reform programmes seek to implement, not neighbourhood states' own conceptions of what their states should be committed to internally. As a result, there is a sense in which 'local ownership' of the process, while seemingly present, is in practice overshadowed by the EU interests, knowledge and power over what counts as a workable 'modern' state in the context of Europe. Relatively little room is left for a meaningful, deep level of partnership or dialogue, conceptually or in practice (see Korosteleva 2011; Kurki 2013).

Critical academics across policy fields of global governance have recently started paying attention to these processes of 'governmentalisation' of populations in target societies. Abrahamsen has analysed the processes of 'self-management' in development aid through partnerships, pointing to the ways in which international financial organizations and development agencies now rely on developing countries to align themselves with their macro-economic programmes through 'partnership' and consultations (Abrahamsen 2000; 2004). Cook and Kothari (2001), reflecting these same interests, call partnership language today's new tyranny in development policy. Joseph (2012) analyses how Western governments and states are equally governmentalised to abide by neoliberal politico-economic demands. The research of the 'Political Economies of Democratisation' project has recorded the role of governmental power relations in the fields of anti-corruption (Gebel 2013), EU democracy promotion (Kurki 2011; 2013) and NGO democracy promotion (Kurki 2013).

What is important to note about these critiques of democratization is that they argue that local contextualization and ownership have marked not the end of power relations in democracy promotion but the shift in techniques of power. Reliance on NGOs and ability to turn to 'locals' reflect a maturation of power projection tools by donors, not their wish to remove power or ideological aims from their work in support of democracy. This is despite the fact that many practitioners themselves often believe the rhetoric of their own frameworks and thus come to glorify local ownership as a paradigm shift of significance. We contend that despite the seeming shifts, 'pedagogy of power' (Teivainen 2009), the tendency to wish to 'tell others' how democracy should be organized, is prevalent in democracy support, even of a locally owned kind.

Conclusion

One of the central paradoxes of democracy support today is that while the idea of democracy is ostensibly encouraged, advocated and, indeed, promoted, at the same time donors try to step away from the responsibility that advocacy of specific values entails. They argue that democracy is today 'locally' contextualized and even contested, and that democracy promotion needs to reflect this by becoming respectful of local ownership. Yet, can one stick by specific values and promote them and see through the principle that all decisions and value systems should be 'locally engendered'. Is there not a contradiction here?

Arguably the contradictions in the very idea of locally owned democracy promotion are played out today in democracy support and assistance. While in many ways the moves in this direction are positive – for locally owned democracy support is surely more democratic and also successful than an imposed democratization – we should not forget that power has not disappeared from democracy promotion. It is still being exercised in implicit and covert, if sometimes unacknowledged and unintentional, ways. This is why local ownership has not ended up producing radical changes in democracy promotion. It is an agenda which is seen as and practiced in ways congruent with the democracy promoters' values and interests: their liberal democratic value prescriptions and their beliefs in liberal politico-economic orders in target countries. Even though 'no model' seems evident in democracy promotion today, even locally owned democracy may amount to the promotion of a 'model'. Many critical theorists argue that this model is an essentially neoliberal one. While democratization can be locally owned and exercised, it should be primarily democratization which does not challenge the principles of open markets, open state-challenging civil society, electoral and constitutional liberal democracy and entrepreneurial exercise of rights by rational individuals. This kind of democratization is valuable and important; yet, it is undeniably only one interpretation of what democratization could mean (see Kurki 2013).

Notes

1. 'Asian values' are considered to include a preference for collectivism and societal harmony, as opposed to individualism and competition associated with Western 'liberal' ideals.
2. *Acquis communautaire* is a French term referring to the cumulative body of European Community laws, comprising the EC's objectives, substantive rules, policies and, in particular, the primary and secondary legislation and case law – all of which form part of the legal order of the European Union (Eurofound 2013).

6 Is democracy promotion limited to achieving political reform or does it aim to advance liberal economic reform?

To ask such a provocative question boils down to an analysis of what is actually promoted in contemporary democracy promotion. Is democracy promotion limited to political assistance such as supporting the creation of an institutional framework that allows for the practice of democratic politics? Or does democracy promotion go beyond a focus on the political to include practices that also influence the organization of the economy in countries receiving democracy assistance? What we are concerned with here is not the range of democracy promotion practices as such (as described in Chapter 2), but rather the (often implicit) consequences for economic structures of countries subjected to democracy promoters' attempts to shape the nature of the political realm. The interest in economic dimensions of democracy promotion arises from the fact that many critics of democracy promotion highlight that democracy promotion is, in fact, more about the safeguarding and promotion of economic interests and ideals than it is about 'democracy' as a political value per se. William Robinson (1996), for example, has argued that US democracy promotion is nothing more and nothing less than an attempt by specific capitalist elites to structure the economies of developing states in line with (neo)liberal principles which seek to open the economies of the affected countries to the global capitalist interests.

The positions of practitioners on the links between the political and the economic spheres vary. Classically the position has been to separate the economic and the political. Practitioners have emphasized that democracy promotion – the attempt to institute open elections and multi-party systems – has nothing to do with economic agendas as such. Yet, today, in the context of the financial crisis and also the failure of many countries to democratize in the context of liberal open market economies, many democracy promoters have been led to take a more nuanced view. Many now argue that, 'yes', economic reform is crucial for democratic reform to succeed and vice versa. Yet, the actors conceive of the relationship between economic and political reform in different ways. Some explicitly argue for economic liberalization, such as many US agencies; others, such as the EU and many NGOs, argue for somewhat more subtle recognition of complex inter-linkages between development and democracy.

We argue here that democracy promotion does indeed always concern the economic dimension. Any separation of the economic and political realms is artificial and misleading, for which political values are active in a specific regime has an effect on how the economy is structured. However, we argue that when trying to deal with the complex relationships between economic reform and democracy, democracy promoters should better recognize that economic agendas often emerge from democracy promotion today in subtle ways and, crucially, in ways which still tend to favour liberal economic developmental models.

We proceed in making our claims in three steps. First, we examine the reasons for the association of economic liberalism with democracy promotion. Second, we then examine how democracy promoters have sought to distance themselves from economically liberal ideals, often through separating realms of the political and the economic. We argue that this separation is unpersuasive and cosmetic and indeed today democracy promotion is always about the economy. Third, the crucial question in the contemporary democracy promotion landscape is: how should the economy and the political interact exactly in democracy promotion? Here we argue that this needs to be considered further. The liberal position on the role of the economy is a problematic one: alternative politico-economic ideas need to be considered. Those actors that see the economic and the political as interlinked still tend to lean – implicitly or explicitly – towards liberal developmental ideals. We argue that a clearer understanding of extra-liberal politico-economic alternatives – reform liberal or social democratic – can benefit how democracy promoters conceive of the interaction of economy and politics (Kurki 2013).

Promoting democracy and free markets

Many critics (examined in more detail in Chapters 3 and 7) have pointed to the deep role that liberal economic ideas play in democracy promotion. Why are they concerned with economic liberalism when it comes to democracy promotion? Is democracy not a purely political ideal, without influence on economic trajectories of states?

The reason this issue has arisen is that amongst some of the key democracy promoters, for some time, democratization has been a goal intricately attached to the idea of liberal economic reform. The Reagan and Clinton administrations, for example, always closely linked open market reform and democracy (Smith 2007; 2012). Indeed, this position is still influential in the US where democracy promotion entails and goes hand in hand with economic liberalization.

This understanding is grounded in the domination of modernization theory and institutional capacity building as the two main approaches that inform policy debates on foreign aid. Modernization theory argues that democracy is the result of social and economic transformation through the generation of economic growth (Krasner 2011: 124–5). And such generation of economic wealth relies on the adoption of free market principles by recipient countries.

An examination of the discourses on democracy promotion in the US, but also among some other actors, shows clearly that the promotion of open economy is usually associated with programmes of political liberalization. Free market economy provides a structural underpinning to political liberalization. A free market economy driven by a dynamic private sector is the best option for countries that wish to modernize and secure human development for their societies. The promotion of liberal democracy and free market economy are inseparable and critical for mutual success. Liberal democracy as a political regime and capitalism as an economic system work hand in hand and support each other's objectives.

For example, when Secretary of State Hilary Clinton defines the concept of free nation, she highlights three mutually supportive essential elements: 'representative government, a well-functioning market, and civil society [which together] work like three legs of a stool. They lift and support nations as they reach for higher standards of progress and prosperity' (Clinton 2010). Democracy and human development are mutually reinforcing in such a discourse. But in fact, all of these elements are seen as indispensable to the survival of recently formed democratic governments, which need to be shielded from violence caused by social and economic inequality (Clinton 2009). Clinton sees human rights, democracy and development as three contingent objectives with agendas that should be designed and implemented cooperatively.

Similarly, the United States Agency for International Development (USAID), the agency in charge of the bulk of US democracy promotion programmes, adopts a similar discourse on the complementarity between democracy and free markets. This is seen as the most efficient combination to allow developing countries to progress, but also, in favour of US national interests. There are very active and comprehensive programmes that target the development of the private sector through private-public partnerships and financial aid at work in USAID. Administrator Rajiv Shah recently explained the rationale to support developing countries' development: 'our assistance also derives benefits for the American people: it keeps our country safe and strengthens our economy' (Shah 2011: 6), and, 'to win the future, we must continue to reach developing world consumers through innovative business models and targeted assistance, accelerating the peaceful rise of the markets they represent' (Shah 2011: 10).

For all the discourses on human rights, democratic values, and plurality of recipients of aid, US democracy promotion seems to be driven by a model of politico-economic development dominated by economic considerations. This approach, which stems from the belief that free markets drive economic development, posits economic growth and democracy as main drivers of development. In such a model, the political sphere is seen as responsible for the generation of conditions conducive to development through economic growth.

Thus, USAID is not in a position to implement democracy promotion programmes that limit the scope of action of economic actors in their quest to develop the private sector in developing countries, because, the argument goes, a buoyant private sector is a key to successful development, and a market for American goods and services. In practice, such political and economic liberalization rests on a close association between the political and the economic spheres; the political mediates in the direction of greater economic openness. Political liberalization thus means to build representative institutions that organize the exercise of democracy, but also the creation of an institutional and value-based framework that facilitate the penetration for free market economy in developing societies and the preservation of social stability (Kurki 2013).

Box 6.1 Millennium Challenge Corporation and free market

The role of free market in US thinking on democracy promotion is made clear by an analysis of the Millennium Challenge Corporation (MCC), an independent US government aid agency that posits good governance, economic freedom and investment in developing countries' citizens at the centre of its aid philosophy. Indeed, MCC argues that development relies on economic growth and democracy: 'strong democratic institutions are some of the very institutions which enable sustainable, locally owned, positive economic outcomes' (MCC 2007: ii). The MCC almost defines the relationship between the political and the economic spheres as symbiotic: 'We [MCC] are acting consciously on the belief that democracy and economic development are not competing aims, but rather fully complimentary objectives' (MCC 2007: ii). Such principles of development aid identify democratic institutions as facilitators of the operations of a free market economy: just and democratic governance means to promote political pluralism, equality and the rule of law; respect human and civil rights; protect private property rights; encourage transparency and accountability of governments; and combat corruption. In addition to democratic rule, the MCC argues that economic freedom is the best guarantor of economic growth. Hence, countries that enter a compact with MCC must develop policies that encourage firms and citizens to participate in global trade and international capital markets, promote private sector growth, and strengthen market forces in the economy, but also respect workers' rights including the right to form labour unions (MCC 2011: 5–6). What MCC strives for is to create political, legal and social conditions that secure social stability, which is indispensable for the operations of a free market economy.

But just because some agencies involved in democracy promotion argue that economic liberalization is essential to democracy, this does not mean that all democracy promoters have always embraced economic liberalization. In fact, many have long distanced themselves from such economic aims. Let us examine this position in more detail.

Separating the political from the economy

There are democracy promotion actors that conceptualize their work as political in essence. The focus of such democracy promotion practitioners is on the facilitation of the emergence of democratic societies in non-democratic countries or post-authoritarian countries in transition. This assistance in creating the conditions for a democratic society to emerge relies on programmes that target democratic actors and processes. Hence, democracy assistance focuses on support to democratic political parties, civil society organizations that constitute the social fabric of a nascent democracy, and the processes through which they can aggregate and express their interests and values. The economic dimension of liberalization is thus not conceived explicitly as part of, or as linked to, the work of such democracy promoters. This does not mean that these actors do not take into consideration the role played by economic rights – and potentially their social benefits – in democracy promotion work. They are aware of socio-economic rights, but tend to focus on the solidly internationally recognized body of political and human rights. Thus, the National Endowment for Democracy (NED) for example, focuses its work on political and civil rights and on building democratic institutions in the countries NED assists (Bridoux and Kurki 2012). This is despite the fact that the NED is aware that political, social and economic rights tend to overlap. The link between the political and economic dimensions of liberalization is not explicitly made in most of its work as the focus remains on the facilitation of democratization in the political realm (Bridoux and Kurki 2012).

Further, for many practitioners attached to political foundations and NGOs, for example, the lessons with regard to the political effects of hard-nosed economic liberalization are well-taken. Given that it is acknowledged that economic liberalization can bring with it serious problems for the processes of democratization (see, for example, Abrahamsen 2000), many democracy promoters explicitly seek to distance themselves from the kind of liberal structural adjustment policies that were dominant in the 1980s and 1990s. In response to the association of democracy promotion with economic liberalization viewed sceptically amongst the target populations of democracy promotion, these actors have sought to emphasize that, for them, democracy is first and foremost a political regime. Once political democratization has been achieved it is up to populations in transition countries to freely decide on their economic future. It is not for democracy promoters to impose economic models. As a result, work has focused on the more 'neutral' process of political liberalization: constitution-building, electoral processes, political party training, civil society development.

This position which seeks to separate the economic from the political reform processes is, we argue, problematic. This is because, from our perspective, informed by critical sensitivities, any separation between the economic and the political is actually rather artificial. The critical literature develops an alternative, which highlights the subtle intertwining of economic and political agendas.

For example, critical theorists challenge the separation of the political and economic dimensions in democracy promotion through specifically condemning the purposive promotion of *a low-intensity democracy* – or polyarchy – by Western governments (Robinson 1996: 6–7; Gills and Rocamora 1992; Gills *et al.* 1993). Promotion of low-intensity democracy, or polyarchy, is, they argue, an instrument of global capitalist forces, which seek to dominate popular masses and limit their aspirations for an extensive democratization of social and economic life. What they mean by low-intensity democracy is a democratic system in which there is a purposive separation of the political from the economic. Indeed, a crucial characteristic of such a democratic system is the limitation of political action to the political dimension, and hence, the separation of the socioeconomic order from the political. The meaning of democracy is thus limited to its institutional dimension. Democracy is an ensemble of 'institutional arrangements for arriving at political decisions in which individuals acquire the power to decide by means of a competitive struggle for the people's votes' (Schumpeter 1947: 269).

Box 6.2 NED and political democracy

The National Endowment for Democracy is an organization representative of an approach to democracy promotion where the focus is squarely on influencing the political processes in target countries, even as the role of economy in influencing political development is acknowledged.

Funded by the US Congress, NED is a non-governmental organization that funds, in the first instance, four core affiliated organizations: two institutes affiliated respectively to the Republican and Democratic parties; the International Republican Institute (IRI), the National Democratic Institute (NDI); and the American Center for International Labor Solidarity (ACILS), and the Center for International Private Enterprise (CIPE).

NED's goal consists in mobilizing private citizens and groups in the United States to design and implement programmes in collaboration with those abroad who wish to foment democratic futures for their countries; 'to help others build democratic institutions and strengthen democratic processes that will promote individual rights and freedoms' (NED, undated). Thus NED, 'guided by the NED Act, which authorizes Congressional funding for its work, functions as a private and vigorously independent institution that has as its sole mission support for democracy. NED is primarily a grant-making institution, and it seeks out newly-emerging groups in both democratizing and authoritarian countries around the world, helping to empower the most effective grassroots activists' (NED 2012: 7).

NED's understanding of its mission relies on several postulates that shape the type of activities the organization undertakes: 1. NED's work advances US national interest; 2. democratization is a long-term process; 3. a democratic system can take various forms depending on local realities and hence does not have to follow the US or any other particular model; 4. democracy grows from within societies and cannot be exported. Further, and what is of significance to us here, NED also acknowledges the role of a liberal economy as an important 'prerequisite of a democratic political system' (NED undated; 2007; 2012). Nevertheless, the core focus of its activities remains the political system and civil society.

For NED political pluralism is essential to the development of democracy. 'A variety of independent organized groups representing diverse interests' (NED, undated) all contribute to the flourishing of a free and fair competition for power in the society undergoing democratization. Vigorous private organizations also constitute a check to unwarranted expansion of governmental power through the representation and defence of the rights of their members.

Indeed, deeply embedded in NED's understanding of political and economic liberalization seems to be a classical liberal defence of limited intervention of the state in economic affairs, for fear that 'big government will limit private enterprise' (Bridoux and Kurki 2012). The ideal of representative institutions and effective civil society as key drivers of democratization remains at the heart of NED's conception of democracy promotion. In this sense, even though NED is aware that there is an economic dimension to democratization, its work focuses mainly on protecting basic political rights, procedures and democratic institution building.

A polyarchical system, Robinson argues, allows for the reconciliation of an obvious paradox in democratic societies: democracy in a society can exist alongside blatant social and economic inequalities generated by capitalism. The key issue in a polyarchy is the stability of the politico-economic order that is controlled by the elites, and hence the question that worries those elites is how to make sure that inequalities do not threaten their dominance: How do elites avert the rise of class war between the haves and have nots? The answer is to present social stability as guaranteed by the use of power in the general interest of society. Consequently, any attempt to question democracy-polyarchy, constitutes a direct attack on the general welfare of the population. In turn, polyarchy eliminates the notion that there could be a contradiction between elite rule and democracy. Therefore, as Robinson argues, 'polyarchy as a distinct form of elite rule performs the function of legitimating existing inequalities, and does so more effectively than authoritarianism' (1996: 51). Democracy, in this case, is a regulatory mechanism applied to intra-societal conflict between groups that seek to achieve specific interests. Political power is thus defined by the distribution of specific resources brought into the political game by interest-groups and by the nature of the institutional arrangements that organize the exercise of power. The problem with the promotion of such a seemingly neutral model of democracy is that while political power originates in the resources and capacity of actors to organize themselves, the distribution of material resources is not organized in the political sphere but in the socioeconomic sphere (Robinson 1996: 53). Robinson's critique is particularly important because it condemns democracy promotion for its intentional separation of the political and economic spheres of liberalization.

We think Robinson is on the right track. There are implications in artificially separating the economic and the political in democracy promotion. We need to be mindful of the ways in which democracy, if implemented in a restricted and narrow liberal way, may end up encouraging particular forms of democratization, forms which may undermine or contradict the wishes of the population. Thus, for example, as Abrahamsen (2000) demonstrates in her analysis of democracy promotion in Africa, the wishes of the populations for social democratic forms of governance, concerned with social and economic justice, can be made unfeasible in the context of the promotion of *liberal* forms of democratization by external actors.

Indeed, from a *critical perspective*, which emphasizes the multiplicity of consequences of seemingly neutral conceptual decisions (in this case, democracy being presented as self-evidently political), what is crucial to note is that democracy is not just a politically consequential concept but is in itself also a politico-economically consequential concept. How? It is important to note that when democrats define the scope and modes of democratic decision-making, they also define the relationship between democracy and economic processes and structures. From this perspective, even the liberal politico-economic viewpoint, which is premised on the separation of the economy and politics, is a politico-economic model: to disconnect the political realm from the economy is to make a statement that the economy should be left to its own devices; which in turn supports a free market economy liberated of governmental control. If we do not perceive this, we may come to miss the ways in which the very separation of economy and politics *itself* limits the democratic horizons in respect of the politico-economic possibilities available to populations.

Also, it is crucial to note that if we don't acknowledge that there is a link between particular formulations of democracy and the economy, we also miss the more subtle ways in which power can be exercised through democracy promotion. Indeed, as outlined in Chapter 3, hidden expressions of power with regard to economy as well as politics can be embedded in the seemingly neutral technical aspects of practices of democracy promotion. For example, the EU's regulations on good governance in its neighbourhood, arguably, implicitly specify particular liberal economic developmental visions as well as a specific liberal model of democracy. This is often not noted, because the EU does not like to openly acknowledge which democratic or politico-economic development model it stands for in its neighbourhood policies. Also, in civil society aid, as was argued in Chapter 5, both the US and the EU seem to prefer to work with liberal democratic actors, which also favour the liberal economic model. This favouring of specific kinds of actors can be far from overt and is today increasingly embedded in the mechanisms that operationalize democracy promotion.

For example, the procurement, management and assessment systems that constitute the nuts and bolts of democracy promotion, implicitly and unintentionally, involve the selection by democracy promoters of very specific partners that will benefit from democracy assistance (Kurki 2011). Indeed, those actors that are most able to meet donors' demands for entrepreneurship, accountability and especially financial transparency and reliability, are most likely to receive funds (Crawford and Abdulai 2012).

So it seems that democracy does have economic consequences for developmental trajectories and liberal and neoliberal tendencies tend to – implicitly or explicitly – dominate in democracy promotion frameworks. But if democracy is economically consequential, how exactly should democracy promoters frame the relationship between economy and politics?

Rethinking economy and politics relationship?

It is interesting to note that, in recent years, partly in response to the financial crisis, democracy promoters have started to increasingly acknowledge the interconnections between democracy and the economy, specifically through their intertwining of democracy promotion and development policies. Development is considered necessary to support democracy and democracy development. As a UNESCO report on democracy and development concludes: 'Everyone now agrees that there is a close relationship between democracy and development' (UNESCO 2002).

But as the same report also indicates, the crucial question today is: what is the nature of the links between economic development and democratic progress? How exactly should the economy and the political interact in democracy promotion?

Many scholars, democracy promoters and development practitioners look for answers to these questions. They predominantly do so by trying to trace the effects of democratization on economic development or vice versa (see for example Lipset 1959; Barsh 1992; Przeworski 2000; Cheibub and Vreeland 2010).

This is not the only way to approach the issue, however. The critical approach, which directs us to think seriously about concepts and ideology and also their consequences in terms of power relations, encourages us to pay attention to the fact that there are multiple potential politico-economic visions and models that could serve as the basis for democracy promotion. This view leads us to challenge the 'self-evidence' of a liberal democratic model as well as the association of it with a self-evidently superior liberal economic model.

As has been highlighted, many recipients of democracy promotion do not share the view that there is a singular set of visions that should guide democratization or economic reform. Instead, as Abrahamsen (2000), Robinson (1996), and Gills, Rocamora and Wilson (1993) highlight, many democratic activists aspire to more radical extra-liberal models such as social democracy, participatory democracy or forms of radical democracy. These activists argue that democratic government has to also be able to control the sphere of the economic and to redistribute wealth in such ways that make the equality of opportunity of individuals to exercise their decision-making power in a democracy possible. They argue that a purely liberal model fails to embrace these deeper socio-economic forms of democratization in its eagerness to defend the minimal liberal state or to separate the economic and the political. It is important then, from a critical perspective, to listen to these alternative views. Otherwise, democracy promotion runs the risk of becoming little more than a hegemonic project which imposes particular visions on target societies – an argument which we discuss in more detail in the following chapter.

Also, from a critical perspective, it is important for practitioners and commentators on democracy promotion to remain attuned to the ways in which economic priorities of specific kinds can 'seep out' of democracy promotion, even when democracy promoters try not to influence economic trajectories. As has been seen, even the attempts to separate democracy promotion from economic agendas have failed to properly address the complex relationship, that is, democracy and the economy are intricately interlinked. Democracy promoters, who tend to (sometimes inadvertently) encourage liberal (political and economic) transitions, have failed to offer multiple democratic futures or dialogue as to what kinds of politico-economic systems of democracy might best suit the contexts of the recipients of support.

As has been argued by the authors of this book elsewhere (Kurki 2013), a fuller consideration of alternative politico-economic models – participatory democracy, social democracy or cosmopolitan democracy – is necessary today, partly because the classical liberal tradition is less and less self-evidently the only tradition, but partly because better forms of economic as well as political democracy are needed for democratic systems to deliver for populations. It is not the case that democracy equals liberal democratic market liberalism. One of the challenges of democratization is facilitation of broad and substantive debate about what the exact role of democratic decision-making is in ensuring the autonomy of individuals as 'democratic decision-makers'. Where the balance between democracy and the economy is to be struck is not a simple, but a complex and dialogical matter. Democracy promoters should recognize this and openly encourage broad and multiple traditions of politico-economic democratization.

Conclusions

So is democracy promotion about political reforms only, or is it also about economic reform and, if so, is it about the promotion of economic development of a particular liberal kind? We have argued that yes, democracy promotion is also about economic reform. Some have openly acknowledged this. Others have contested the idea that democratic reform of a political kind need necessitate a particular economic system. We have argued that the attempts to separate the economic and the political fail, as all attempts at democratization also have impacts on the economy. We have also suggested that there is nothing self-evident about the liberal politico-economic alternative, and have suggested that a more fruitful way forward in thinking about the complex relationship might be to think seriously about multiple different ways in which populations and political groups may wish to frame the economy-state relationship.

If democracy is about achieving economic liberalization, in whose interests is it? Arguably, there are real benefits to populations from increased economic activity. Facts seem to indicate that even though some aspects of democracy and free markets promotion are indeed questionable, the promotion of democratic values and open economy did benefit populations of aid recipient countries. An Oxfam report points out that compared to transitioning countries undergoing political and economic liberalization, 'African states in conflict have 50 per cent more infant deaths, 15 per cent more undernourished people, five less years of life expectancy, 20 per cent more adult illiteracy, 2.5 fewer doctors per patient, and 12.4 per cent less food per person on average' (Paris 2010: 353). As Roland Paris contends, wide ranging expressions of 'distrust, pessimism and even cynicism' about the promotion of liberal values in the developing world, are exaggerated.

At the same time, there is little doubt that Western interests are also served by democracy promotion. Robinson and others suggested that democracy promotion is a veneer that hides far more hard-nosed economic interests. It is a tool of the capitalist classes to subjugate people to a model of democracy, which denies the possibility of egalitarian socio-economic progress. Indeed, we have observed that there is a tendency to promote a specific liberal model, which silences those whose aspirations are less self-evidently in line with either liberal democracy or liberal market economics. This is why we have suggested that alternative politico-economic models are at least considered in democracy promotion.

The workings of democracy promotion discussed here seem to indicate that far from emancipating populations, today's democracy promotion sets the foundations for hegemonic relations of power between donors and recipients. Indeed, if as suggested elsewhere and in this chapter, democracy promotion is all about the promotion, and acceptance, of a single politico-economic model that is liberal in nature, then (if there is just one alternative), the relationships constructed in democracy promotion are 'hegemonic' in nature. This is the theme the final chapter of this book turns to.

Notes

1. In a liberal political system there is a tendency to lean towards economically liberal structures with an emphasis on facilitation of economic openness. In contrast in a social democratic system, the balance of economic and political power is different. The political intervenes in how the economy is organized, with values of community and equality shaping the distribution of economic power as well as the political functions of the state.
2. We do not deem it necessary to ask the question of market access through democracy promotion to the work done by international financial institutions. Indeed, the purpose and aim of those institutions is precisely to achieve greater global economic openness. Internation Financial Institution's (IFIs) democracy promotion work is essentially a sidekick of free market promotion policies with the principle of conditionality mediating between the political and economic dimensions of IFI's work.
3. Media, human rights activists, trade unions, business associations, etc.
4. Such as constitution writing, electoral assistance, political parties formation and training, etc.
5. As, for example, lack of attention to domestic institutional conditions as supporting successful democratization and marketixation, underestimation of contradictions between goals of liberalization, lack of coordination between democracy promotion actors involved, lack of resources, deficient knowledge about local conditions and actors, etc. (Paris 2010: 347).

7 Is democracy promotion reflective of and constructive of 'hegemonic' power relations?

This book has aimed to introduce you to a critical theoretical investigation of democracy promotion, guided by a broadly 'critical approach' which is concerned with deeper questions of how ideas and policies are constituted, what their conceptual premises are, and how power relations and hegemony work today. This approach, we have suggested, contributes to analysis of empirical trends in democracy promotion – of interest and values within it but also of analysis of key empirical developments with democracy promotion such as its role in regime change and its context-sensitive credentials. We now wish to conclude on a question that has been of key concern to critical theorists: to what extent, and in what ways, does democracy promotion entail and promote 'hegemonic' social relations in world politics?

To answer this question, this final chapter turns to the work of Antonio Gramsci (1971 [1929–35]) and of critical theorists who apply Gramsci's insights in the workings of social hegemony production at the international level. We also refer to Michel Foucault's theorization of social power relations organizing the 'conduct of conduct' of social actors subjected to the exercise of power (Foucault 2008). We do so because both Gramsci and Foucault, amongst other theorists of power, put the idea that power is expressed explicitly or implicitly through consent generation at the core of their understanding of how power works. We argue here that such an understanding of power based on consent, which in turn leads to hegemonic relationships of power between the powerful and subordinates, is particularly relevant to the way democracy promotion works in today's world. Indeed, as we have shown in the previous chapters, democracy promotion shuns the use of force and instead constitutes a set of policies and instruments that try, explicitly or implicitly, to generate agreement from recipients of democracy promotion on the inherent desirability of liberal democracy as a political regime in the contemporary global order.

Amongst theorists of power and hegemony who applied critical theory to the workings of democracy promotion, it is William Robinson who perhaps most provocatively theorized that role of democracy promotion in the construction of Western hegemony over the international system. As suggested in Chapters 3 and 6, he argued that Western capitalist states' democracy promotion agenda facilitated the construction of a liberal capitalist global order. Such an order would rest on populations being content with electoral liberal democracy, so called 'low intensity democracy', while acceding to the power of capitalist social forces to structure the relations between individuals and state, civil society and global order (Robinson 1996).

Democracy promotion, in this framework, was about the creation of 'consent', or 'hegemony', over visions of 'the good life' amongst populations around the world; it was about moving people away from 'radicalized' socialist or alternative models of development towards recognition of the 'modern' and 'self-evidently superior' credentials of liberal democracy and liberal capitalism for development of societies. These values, however, were promoted, not just because they were superior but because, in fact, they align with the interests of the West, notably Western interests in opening of markets and facilitation of global control over distant populations. Regime change, as Chapter 4 showed, in anything but in name is the end point of democracy promotion – but crucially from Robinson's angle, it is achieved by the creation of consensual hegemony over 'good life' of a specific liberal kind and through the undermining of political and economic contestation to this specific liberal vision (Robinson 1996).

Robinson's account was written in the mid-1990s. How well do these claims still stand? This chapter examines, from the point of view of our critical 'power perspective', the issue of hegemony in world order. We ask to what extent is hegemony being constructed through democracy promotion today? And how does it relate to domination or emancipatory social agendas? The first section of this chapter engages with Robinson's approach to hegemony and suggests that while forms of power are multiple and while consensual construction of hegemony plays a key part in democracy promotion, there are also indications that hegemony today does not function quite as Robinson suggests. Indeed, the second section argues that there are coincidences of interests, adjustments and learning, and new forms of governmental power that play out in democracy promotion, and that in this sense, while hegemony can be identified, it may also be constructed in new and interesting ways and may today generate emancipation but also be subject to more resistance than before, as the third section of the chapter observes.

We argue that democracy promotion today then is not just about 'the West vs. the rest': about Western hegemony over developing nations; rather it is a complex practice which presents some opportunities for emancipatory change, as well as presenting new forms of power relations between donors and recipients, and between political groups within countries receiving democracy assistance aid. Politics, contestation and power are embedded in democracy promotion, we argue: certainly, it is not today, nor was it ever, a 'neutral' technical policy agenda, self-evident in its justifications, aims or methods. Nevertheless, neither is it an agenda that is to be singularly deplored: while many power relations emerge from democracy promotion, so does potential for progressive change. Democracy promotion, too, is a practice which is subject to change and reformulation, a subject which we return to in the conclusion to this book.

Power and hegemony: Dialogue with Robinson

William Robinson (1996), and some of his colleagues, such as Gills, Rocamora and Wilson (1993), have argued that democracy promotion can only be understood as a new form of power projection, as an adjustment to a global power system where support to pliable autocratic regimes no longer fits the rhetoric of the 'democratic' nations. A new tool of control in proxy countries had to be developed in the 1980s given the problems counter-insurgency strategies that sought to support right-wing dictators was creating for the US. Democracy promotion became the tool, Robinson argues, which sought to de-radicalize social forces in developing countries and to align the views and interests of populations subjected to democracy promotion with those of Western powers. Promotion of liberal democracy was a key instrument in the facilitation of stability but at the same time a neoliberal vision of economics, politics and society was delivered via democracy promotion in states where, too often, opposition forces preferred socialist, social democratic or other radical developmental trajectories, often ones which emphasized autonomy and independence from Western actors.

But is it still viable to perceive democracy promotion from this angle, even if this interpretation may have corresponded to the early years of the Reagan administration's actions? In the context of a more global consensus on democracy promotion and the globalization of activity in the promotion and support of democracy (examined in more detail in Chapter 2), can democracy promotion still be perceived as a tool of seeking compliance of target populations? In the context of the many 'learning curves' in democracy promotion, and crucially the shifts towards democracy support and assistance over more assertive practices (examined in more detail in Chapters 4 and 5), can hegemony still be argued to structure democracy promotion activities? How should we, in the light of our approach to power, and our analysis of developments in democracy promotion, analyse hegemony and domination in democracy promotion? What can we conclude on the basis of the discussion in this book?

Firstly, we have observed that democracy is not an apolitical, non-ideological or neutral concept. As a result, when democracy is promoted, specific ideological visions of good life, society and power relations emerge from it. There have been discernible shifts in how the political or ideological content of democracy promotion is communicated. During the 1980s and especially the early 1990s as the Cold War ended, democracy promotion was characterized by the dominance of liberal principles. Since then such a dominance continues but is somewhat diluted following the crisis of the liberal economic order since 2008 and the questioning of the self-evidence of liberal democratic political values in the context of the Arab Spring. It remains the case that ideological preferences as to what the political and economic systems of states should look like are embedded in a whole range of democracy promotion activities of all key actors – The United States, the European Union, non-governmental organizations, International Financial Institutions, and International Organizations (such as the United Nations, the Organization for Security and Co-operation in Europe [OSCE], and the Organization for Economic Co-operation and Development [OECD], for example) (Kurki 2013; Gebel 2012;

Ayers 2006; Crawfôrd and Abdulai 2011). These preferences are liberal and specifically neoliberal in nature.

The embedding of such liberal and neoliberal ideological preferences is a reality, despite the fact that many democracy promoters today recognize the need for a more nuanced language of democracy promotion. Thus, some actors recognize the need to take account of multiple paths to democracy; others even speak of social democratic or reform liberal paths to democratization being facilitated. These more progressive alternatives to the dominance of a liberal and neoliberal discourse in democracy promotion result from the realization by democracy promoters that, in the context of the financial crisis and of the Arab Spring of 2011, democracy is a politico-economic concept. Democracy 'that delivers' is becoming essential, as discussed in Chapter 6. Democracy promotion is not limited to the political dimension and the institutionalization of democratic politics, but increasingly also encompasses an economic agenda.

Interestingly, there are adjustments today in democracy promotion which open up the liberal principles to exploration of different variants of liberal thought. In the EU, for example, more reference has been made to social democratic ideals and even in the US under the Obama administration there has been an increased emphasis on the importance of social and economic justice (Kurki 2013: Ch. 7) Nevertheless, alternative models of democracy – participatory or social democratic – are rarely specifically explored, nor are the challenges which they pose to liberal democratization deeply investigated (Kurki 2013).

In sum, it is crucial to understand here that, even though democracy promotion tends to be presented by its practitioners as a neutral and technical agenda, such an agenda still carries over the ideological seeds of Western hegemony through the communication of specific liberal and neoliberal principles passed on for developing populations to 'consent' on. And this seemingly benign ideological transfer, we argue, in turn, comes to define and structure power relations in societies that are subjected to democracy promotion.

However, and secondly, we can and should note that, while ideological principles still flow from democracy promotion, the use of power in coercive terms is minimal today in democracy promotion, perhaps exactly because its use has been seen to undermine the control of target populations. The 2003 war with Iraq, and the subsequent occupation of the country, was an exception to this rule, and has reinforced the reasons as to why brute force is rarely used in enforcement of democratic aims. Consensual methods – from incentives to civil society assistance – are today the centre-ground of democracy support.

Yet, even so, the threat of the use of force, it can be argued, is still never far away. Indeed, even when more benign and consensual methods are applied – aid conditionality, for example – it is not the case that threats are absent. For example, the withdrawal of economic aid, if democratic progress does not satisfy donors' expectations (discussed in Chapter 4), can be considered as an exercise of coercive power. This aid is important for many aid-dependent states and as such the threat of withdrawal causes potentially existential issues for the stability of the regime in place. It could be argued that even the threat of military intervention is not entirely absent from democracy promotion. If a country does not fall in line with the democracy promoters' wishes they may drift towards confrontation provoking potentially active coercion. Consider, for example, the failure of Gaddafi to meet the expectations of behaving like a democratic leader in Libya in 2011.

Target countries, then, should keep in mind both the consensual incentives to comply and the not-so-consensual threats that may lurk should they decide not to comply. Coercion is arguably never desirable and should be avoided. This general avoidance of coercion, it could be argued, is realized today in democracy promotion. Generation of consent on liberal democracy and the liberal economic model is still the name of the game in democracy promotion.

How do we understand this theoretically? If we turn to Gramsci's understanding of hegemony we have better tools to understand these dynamics in democracy promotion.

Hegemony from a Gramscian perspective

Democracy promotion strategies as we have seen are deployed in two spheres: the public or governmental sphere through the democratization of institutions that organize the exercise of democracy as political regime, and in the civil society, usually identified as the seat of counter-power to the government. In analysing how hegemony is created within a state, considering a Gramscian concept of the state is particularly interesting. Indeed, the state in its broad Gramscian definition consists in the civil society (sphere of private interests) and the political society (state apparatus). Hence, it includes the traditional view of the administrative, executive, and coercive apparatus of government coupled with the underpinnings of the political structure in civil society, elements such as church, the educational system, the press, briefly 'all the institutions which helped to create in people certain modes of behavior and expectations consistent with the hegemonic social order' (Cox 1996: 126). To be successful, hegemonic policies must be deployed in the civil and political society.

From a critical perspective, those democracy promotion strategies that are deployed in the political society are the most visible operations undertaken by democracy promoters. They involve actions like rewriting constitutions, organizing elections, reformatting relations between the executive, legislative and judiciary powers and so on. In contrast, the critical perspective would argue that the strategies in civil society tend to be more discrete and are also more based on consent generation through a succession of overt mechanisms (offering grants for civil society organizations) and covert procedures (the ensemble of expectations attached to attributing money to CSOs). Democracy promotion strategies, it could be argued, are about facilitation of a ground of agreement with the targets of democracy promotion in order to lead those recipients of democracy aid to adopt liberal democracy as a new political regime. The end of democracy promotion is, arguably, to achieve social cohesion through ideological hegemony.

From a Gramscian perspective, democracy promotion can be read as a project that seeks the cooptation of entire elites and populations to specific democratic modes of governance. This cooptation is essentially founded on an agreement between democracy promoters and democracy aid recipients that an alternative to authoritarianism is desirable. It is an open and conscious interactive process. However, the stability of the new democratic pact requires less visible ideological forms of power that are inherent to the creation of a new common identity between donors and recipients. As Gramsci says, a hegemonic relationship is an interactive process as the potential hegemon has to present its policies as being in the interests of the targeted subordinate actor(s). It has to incorporate the subordinate's interests and accordingly make the necessary concessions in its programme for hegemony in order to obtain the consent of the less powerful: 'The hegemony of a class consists in its ability to represent the "universal" interests of the whole of society and to unite to itself a group of allies' (Showstack Sassoon 1982: 111).

Accordingly, from a Gramscian perspective there is a continuous interplay between hegemon and targeted subordinate actor(s) aiming at the identification, aggregation and incorporation of subordinates' vital interests into the hegemon's policies. This is what Gramsci calls a historical bloc, at the core of his notion of hegemony and defined as:

> Structures and superstructures form an 'historical bloc'. That is to say the complex, contradictory and discordant ensemble of the superstructures is the reflection of the ensemble of the social relations of production. (Gramsci 1971: 366)

The historical bloc is brought to existence by the presence of a hegemonic social class. Its main function is to maintain cohesion and identity within the bloc through the prop-agation of a common culture. A social class is hegemonic if it manages to bring the subordinated masses to agree to its own ideas, values and interests, and more im-portantly, if it manages to present them as universal, meaning that they appear in the general interest of the diverse social formations on which hegemony is implemented. This implementation takes place by giving some satisfaction to the subordinate groups while not jeopardizing the interests of the ruling class (Cox 1996: 132).

It can be argued that democracy promotion seeks to achieve the making of such a historical bloc; an agglomeration of interests cemented in uncontested demo-cratic values across democratizing political and civil societies. A new democratic culture provides the canvas on which new democratic institutions and values are sketched. Today's Western democracy promoters can be interpreted as Gramsci's dominant class and recipients of democracy aid can be considered as Gramsci's subordinated masses. Thus conceived, democracy promoters attempt to 'hege-monize', to co-opt elites and populations of target states in their quest to spread liberal democracy globally. To do so, they can rely on a specific cast: those democratic civil society activists that are co-opted as flag bearers of democracy and a new generation of bureaucrats who organize and consolidate the exercise of democracy as political regime across the institutions of democratizing countries. Gramsci would have called them 'organic intellectuals'. We could also call them 'organic democrats'.

But how does this co-option work exactly? A historical bloc requires what Gramsci terms 'organic intellectuals' whose role is to cement the links between structures and superstructures:

> Every social group ... creates together with itself, organically, one or more strata of intellectuals which give it homogeneity and an awareness of its own function not only in the economic but also in the social and political fields. (Gramsci 1971: 5)

So, intellectuals are organically connected with a social class. They produce ideology but also organize it. Indeed, they theorize the ways in which the hegemony can be developed or maintained (Gill 1986: 210). Intellectuals are in charge of the formulation of a message susceptible to gain the consent of subordinated groups to the ruling class's ideology and of the organization and running of the governmental apparatus. These two functions correspond to the dual composition of the superstructure: civil society (private sphere) and political society (the state), corresponding to the two functions of hegemony exercised throughout society and direct domination through the governmental apparatus. As Gramsci explains:

> The intellectuals are the dominant group's 'deputies' exercising the subaltern functions of social hegemony and political government. These comprise: 1. The 'spontaneous' consent given by the great masses of the population to the general direction imposed on social life by the dominant fundamental group; this consent is 'historically' caused by the prestige (and consequent confidence) which the dominant group enjoys because of its position and function in the world of production. 2. The apparatus of state coercive power, which 'legally' enforces discipline on those groups who do not 'consent' either actively or passively. (Gramsci 1971: 12)

When applied to democracy promotion, the paragraph above could be re-written as follows:

> Democracy promoters are liberal democracy's deputies trying to generate consent in the civil and political society of democracy aid target states to the adoption of democracy as political regime. This mission involves: 1. The 'spontaneous' consent given by the elite and populations of target states to a democratic direction imposed on their societies by Western democracy promoters; this consent is caused by a historical political and economic record of liberal democracies considered as more efficient than autocracies. 2. The apparatus of overt and covert techniques of democratic progress and control that 'legally' enforces discipline on those who resist the advance of liberal democracy.

The main function, from this perspective, of democracy promoters is to co-opt 'organic democrats' in target states. They become the 'organically'-linked thinking and organizing elements of new democracies. Their main function, from this viewpoint, is to direct the ideas and aspirations of their populations by forging, as they do for the whole society, a common identity; an identity shared by liberal democrats across the world.

Earlier in this chapter we surveyed the contributions of Robinson's account of democracy promotion as a form of hegemony. Our own Gramscian reading points in the same direction as that of Robinson: democracy promotion could indeed be interpreted as a form of consent-building to the hegemony of liberal democracy, even if the actors of democracy promotion are, today, more plural and multi-faceted than Robinson accepted. The globalization of hegemony does not change the ideological form of democracy promotion, even if it has shifted its language and methods (Kurki 2013). But are there aspects of democracy promotion that this approach, with its emphasis on co-option and consent, does not take into account? Potentially, it is the case. Indeed, we suggest that co-option and consent-building today functions in ways which can be fruitfully 'got at' through the idea of 'governmentality'.

New developments in democracy promotion

One of the key developments we have referred to here has been the evolution of more dispersed and technical managerial functions and modes of democracy promotion. In Chapters 4 and 5, for example, we have emphasized the shift to 'locally owned' and 'self-managed' forms of democracy promotion. Less and less directed, but also less and less 'intentional' and 'planned' control over target populations is taking place in democracy promotion today, as institution-shaping and strict conditionalities have given way to incentive structures and self-managed projects. How do these developments fit with the idea of hegemony construction?

They fit surprisingly well. What is crucial to note about Gramscian ideas on hegemony is that they do not require there to be 'conscious' class strategies per se; they allow for the unconscious or unintentional construction of hegemonies, that is, actions taken by individuals to 'better' societies without the intent of 'controlling' or 'manipulating' them. Construction of hegemony can be non-strategic and still serve the purposes of particular classes or groups of individuals more than others. Indeed, it is exactly these forms of less and less intentional control that we see taking over in democracy promotion today.

It is also these less and less intentional forms of power which other groups of theorists have theorized succinctly. The Foucauldian 'governmentality' literature has specifically tried to theorize how techniques of management can in and of themselves become forms of control and ideological subordination. Foucault's thought on neoliberal governmentality, for example, pointed out that power in today's society seems to emanate from techniques of government where it is exactly the 'self-management' of individuals over their own thoughts and actions which is at the heart of the construction of particular types of social order. 'Entrepreneurial' and 'liberal' 'freedom-safeguarding' individuals stand at the heart of an advanced neoliberal society. It is arguably exactly these sorts of individuals, and not just states, that democracy promotion seeks to bring to life. Appreciation of 'freedom of the individual' and creation of individuals who willingly control and check the state and its power is what stands at the heart of the idea of 'liberal democracy'. It is exactly these types of individuals who make 'social democracy' or 'socialist' systems less and less possible, as they push democracy towards the mould of 'liberal democracy' compatible with free market economy.

Emancipation and resistance

But what does this mean for the emancipatory potential of democracy promotion? If there are only specific kinds of 'properly democratic' actors (i.e. liberal actors) that democracy promoters wish to work with, who does democracy promotion emancipate? Can democracy promotion today claim to facilitate the emancipation of all sections of populations of target states, even those that do not perceive liberal principles to be conducive to their interests? If democracy promotion does not allow for alternatives to the creation of a hegemonic liberal politico-economic system expressed through liberal democracy and free market economy, then can it really be the tool of emancipation of individuals? This is a tricky question.

In our view it is important to appreciate the fact that just because power is at play in societies, and in democracy promotion, this does not mean that freedoms or even emancipation of certain types cannot be realized. Indeed, we would contend that liberalization of societies does, by most measures, assist and facilitate the realization of improvement of social conditions for many individuals. Thus, contrary to many of the critics who imply that democracy promotion, in its often thoroughly liberal forms, is little but a negative and oppressive force, we would point the reader towards careful consideration of the ways in which liberal rights and freedoms expose space for critique, dialogue and debate and provide the conditions for the fulfilment of not only individual rights for self-expression but shared communal feeling of ownership over decision-making. Despite the dangers and instabilities caused, there are many worse things inflicted on people in the world today than liberal democracy. And it should not be forgotten that some of the most well-liked governments and systems are liberal democratic, at least in part.

Yet, while freedom can become exercised as a result of the liberalization of political and economic realms, the critical approach also reminds us that we need to be mindful of the systems of power which may simultaneously be bound up with emancipation of individuals. We need to understand the ways in which democracy promotion can come to control and delimit the kinds and types of freedoms that individuals can exercise or even perceive as relevant to their social conditions. Thus, while liberal democratization arguably improves the lot of many in Egypt today, other types of democratization ideals, social democratic facilitation of welfare rights or Islamic forms of solidarity, become at the same time pushed to the margins. This means that some sectors of society not only 'perceive' liberal democracy as more attractive than others, but also stand to benefit from it more than others, in facilitation of their vision of 'good life'. Emancipation is possible, but always also creates forms of oppression or domination with it.

This is ultimately why recognition of hegemony and its functioning in societies and in democracy promotion is so essential – for without understanding its role, we also may easily become blinded to the forms of delimitation and conditioning which particular hegemonies bring about. We also remain blind to the potential of conflict, contestation and difference in societies, and between societies, as 'false universalisms' become attractive frameworks of reference.

In the absence of emancipation, we should not be surprised to see resistance to democracy promotion and the liberal project. Indeed, interestingly, it would be a mistake to believe that to those actors liberalism does not co-opt remain inactive. Non-liberal and extra-liberal actors that are not supported by liberal democracy promoters constitute knots of resistance to the liberal project in developing societies. Thus, one of the unexpected side effects of hidden liberal expressions of power – the attempt to control the conduct of local actors of politico-economic liberalization – is the generation of sometimes very serious resistance to the liberal project. We examine these forms of resistance in the case study section that follows.

Resistance to the liberal project: the case of Iraq

The occupation and reconstruction of Iraq from 2003 arguably constitutes a case of post-conflict reconstruction and democracy promotion that seems to provide ammunition for William Robinson's theory of polyarchy as facilitator of capitalist advances in developing countries. Cohorts of scholars have criticized the US adventurism in Iraq as essentially a neoliberal project that had little consideration for the welfare of the Iraqi people and their aspirations to freedom and democracy (Bridoux 2011a; Dodge 2010; Harvey 2003; 2007; Herring and Rangwala 2006; Juhasz 2006; Kiely 2005). Did such a project succeed? Was the United States in a position to impose what Dodge calls 'kinetic neoliberalism' (2010) on the Iraqi elite and population? Did the United States manage to impose its hegemony on the Iraqi elite and population?

We argue that, despite the hegemonic project, the implementation did not translate into a hegemonic reality, that is, the adoption by Iraqi elites and population of the norms of liberal democracy and neoliberal economics. Although a shell of democratic decision-making was put in place, this did not translate into the local population embracing liberal values.

This is because the Iraqi political society proved less amenable to obey US orders than anticipated. There is a case to be made that the US failed to win over the Iraqi civil society essentially because of its inability to get the Iraqi elite to adhere to the US project for Iraq. This was mainly due to the establishment of a classical model of electoral democracy and its focus on quick elections between competing parties, which in turn led to an entrenchment of rivalries between Iraq's political factions. Such an approach thus led to a spill-over of the contest for the state in the Iraqi civil society, with political factions engaged in a struggle for support in a bid to stay in, or gain more, power. The absence of a more compre-hensive liberal democratic future for the Iraqi state, which would have addressed critical social and economic issues instead of a focus on the struggle for votes, led to political organizations invading civil society in an attempt to provide services that should have been provided by the state – if it was running – in exchange for electoral support. Despite the attempt to liberalize Iraq, in practice there was little room for the US to cultivate liberal values in Iraqi civil society.

Box 7.1 The failure of the US hegemonic project to win the battle for civil society in Iraq

As Kerr (2009) argues, civil society in post-totalitarian context is weak and subjected to the return of a strong state. In Iraq, this translated into the loss of autonomy of the Iraqi civil society with the rise of faith-based organizations sponsored by political parties in search of legitimacy within the civil society. Such organizations provided healthcare, education and various social services with the intent to gain support for the political parties they were affiliated with. The growing importance of these faith-based 'NGOs' impeded the freedom of action of independent liberal civil society organizations that traditionally, in a liberal democracy, constitute the seat of counter-power to the state. In fact, Kerr argues that the growing presence of faith-party-based civil society organizations could lead civil society organizations to fail 'to consolidate sufficient autonomy to contest or guide the state' (Kerr 2009: 23).

Moreover, liberal organizations are also in direct competition with foreign capitalist economic actors that seek new market shares in Iraq. If, as for example, the transnational capitalist argument goes (Robinson 2004), Iraqi elite are indeed global neoliberal actors, it can be expected that international capitalist interests would be protected and advanced in Iraq. Yet, this is far from being the case. Political parties and religious organizations turned into economic actors that provided services and goods, and thus deprived the private sector of profits. Those profits are then used by their own political organizations to consolidate and expand their power across Iraqi society. In fact, the penetration of a US-led hegemonic neoliberal project in Iraq was not facilitated, but was essentially contested and resisted actively by the majority of the Iraqi elite and population. The sectarian realities that divide Iraqi society are at the forefront of the political debate. Democratic advances in Iraq are limited less by a US-backed plan to promote liberal democracy in complement to neoliberal economic policies, than by the struggle between Iraqi political actors to win over the battle for civil society. The US consistently failed to generate consent to its hegemonic project in Iraqi political and civil society, and did not manage to see off Iraqi resistance to its hegemony.

Such a resistance to the US project of limited democracy from Iraqi political elite and civil society was also replicated in the economic dimension of the liberalization of Iraq. Indeed, far from being for sale, Iraq repulsed early US attempts to open the Iraqi economy to neoliberalism. Although critics often point to greed by global capitalist actors as a key reason for intervention, it is important to nuance any such arguments in three ways. Firstly, such analyses bypass the limitations imposed by the context of the intervention and the US self-awareness that neo-imperial policies – such as the control over Iraqi natural resources – would generate tremendous resistance by Iraqis and condemnation by the international community.

Secondly, critiques underestimated the dire security conditions that impeded market access by foreign interests. Thirdly, those critiques misjudged the degree of resistance to the neoliberal project displayed by the Iraqi political and civil society.

Box 7.2 The failure of the neoliberal project in Iraq

There is no doubt that Coalition Provisional Authority (CPA) orders 12 (trade liberalization) and 39 (regulation of foreign investments) sought to open the Iraqi economy to foreign investments, which was identified as a legitimate step in the direction of foreign ownership of natural resources, including oil. However, while order 39 opens the Iraqi markets to foreign investments, ownership of Iraqi natural resources is specifically forbidden in the text: 'Foreign investment may take place with respect to all economic sectors in Iraq, except that foreign direct and indirect ownership of the natural resources sector involving primary extraction and initial processing remains prohibited' (CPA 2003). Moreover, Foreign Direct Investments (FDIs) in Iraq were limited for an extended period of time (Allawi 2007: 125; Bridoux 2011a: 112; GAO 2005). Until an improvement in stability thanks to 'The Surge' from 2007 onwards, foreign investments, which were supposed to bolster the Iraqi private sector, did not meet expectations. Yet, since 2009, foreign direct investments did rise significantly, essentially thanks to 'a handful of multi-billion dollar energy deals that are the first wave of investments as Iraq moves to develop its hydro-carbon industries' (Dunia Frontier Consultants 2009: 2).

Another critique linked to foreign investments argues that reconstruction contracts were attributed to US firms instead of Iraqi firms. There is ample documentation that confirms a preferential regime for US companies on the basis of US-perceived efficiency of local contractors, identified as unable to perform complex high-tech reconstruction projects. However, it is important to note that, even when Iraqi contractors could have proved a better option in low technology-high labour intensive cases, thanks to their cheaper fees, they rarely won the contracts. As the US Government Accountability Office (GAO) points out, the conditions in Iraq and the lack of contract oversight leads to 'fraud, waste and abuse' (GAO 2007a: 2) and hinders the reconstruction effort (GAO 2007b; 2008). There is no questioning that the US administration attributed major infrastructure contracts to American companies as a form of return on investment in the invasion and occupation. However, legislative developments in Iraq do not seem to support the uncontrolled insertion of global capitalism there.

In fact, as early as 2006, in an attempt to deflect criticism of neo-imperial policies in Iraq, the US government implemented the Iraqi First Act. The Act supported local businesses through developing skills and business practices to enhance Iraqi competitiveness. This led 53 state-owned companies to restart their activities. Overall, by June 2007, Iraqi companies had won contracts with the US government for a total of $1 billion – representing 42 per cent of all contracts awarded (MNF-I 2007). Moreover, in 2006, a new Investment Law replaced CPA Order 39. Far from comprehensively opening the Iraqi economy to foreign direct investments, this law regulated investments in the housing sector. Oil and gas extraction and production, and the bank and insurance sectors were not included in this first Iraqi-made legislation on economic liberalization. Instead of an uncontrolled opening of Iraqi economy to foreign interests, it seems that privatization at work in Iraq was rather selective and less driven by international capitalism than by the need to develop the infrastructure critical to the provision of essential services and to secure revenues for the government. Iraq has grown impatient at the lack of regular electricity provision and running water (Shadid 2010). Iraq needs foreign investments and skills to provide for her population and hence to contribute to an amelioration of the security situation by mitigating discontentment. Thus, one can argue that the opening of the Iraqi economy finds its dynamics domestically more than in an external imposition of neoliberal economic policies by the US. The hegemony of international capitalist forms of social reproduction faces saturation in Iraq due to the local realities affecting the post-war reconstruction process.

In conclusion, there is no doubt that the promotion of democracy in Iraq went hand-in-hand with the promotion of classic neoliberal policies. Yet, we argue, even though those policies intended to open Iraq to global capitalism, local political and economic realities actually dictated the pace of economic liberalization of the country. Far from an outrageous and uncontrolled opening of Iraqi markets to neoliberal forces, we witnessed a more measured liberalization that reflected political interests at stake. The US-led capitalist elite has not taken control of Iraq but, instead, battles local groups representing various religious, ethnic, political and economic interests. The Iraqi case shows that it is necessary to exercise caution in analyses of democracy promotion's drive to not only politically liberalize but also economically open target countries to facilitate their integration in the global economy. The intellectual dominance of modernization theory in official foreign aid circles makes liberal democracy and free market a likely couple. However, it seems vital to analyse carefully the conditions in which those policies of political and economic liberalization are enacted. Indeed, the Iraq case shows that one should not underestimate the power of resistance of local actors when they are faced with Western-initiated reconstruction of their political, social and economic institutions. Even in the face of formidable odds – capitalist forces can be very persuasive – recipients of democracy and free market promotion do retain some autonomy and manage to negotiate, up to a point, the political and economic future of their country. It is true that democracy promotion fairly systematically attempts to open target countries to neoliberal interests. It is less true that it manages to do so successfully at all time. Consequently, one needs to carefully assess narratives of Western hegemony through democracy promotion. Such hegemony is not systematically successful.

Conclusion

We argue here that hegemonies are created and continue to be created through democracy promotion. Particular 'common sense' about what 'democracy' is and what its ideal conditions are is inevitably advanced through democracy promotion, and also the more consensual forms of democracy support. When democracy is supported or assisted, it is always inevitably particular understandings of democracy's meaning which are passed on and encouraged. While this is positive and potentially emancipatory, it is also at the same time delimiting for the kinds of horizons of good life which can be observed. In this sense then democracy promotion is both about power – overt and covert – and also about improvement of life. It is negotiation of these difficult waters of power and emancipation that stands at the heart of the challenges faced today in attempting to 'rethink' and 'redirect' democracy promotion's practice, a topic we turn to in the following concluding chapter in the context of the Arab Uprising of 2010–2011.

Notes

1. The more aggressive democracy promotion policies of the G.W. Bush administration, and the subsequent backlash experienced in the wake of the occupation and attempted liberal nation-building projects in Afghanistan and Iraq, have caused a toning down of democracy promotion rhetoric and practices (Carothers 2008; 2009a; 2012; Diamond 2008a; 2008b; 2008c).
2. In the aftermath of the uprising in Benghazi, Gaddafi decided to use violence to quell the rebels in Libya. This amounted to a contravention of the expectation by the West that Gaddafi should be more conciliatory with those contesting his power.
3. The ensemble of economic relations.
4. The ethical political sphere.

Conclusions

Rethinking democracy promotion

Since December 2010, the Middle East and North Africa has been going through a period of transition, a process that is commonly referred to as the Arab Spring or Arab Uprising. Pro-democracy rebellions against tyrannical regimes spread from Tunisia and Egypt and affected most countries in the region with varying intensity. The Arab Spring constitutes a sizeable challenge for democracy promoters, who have been caught off guard. The revolts questioned the rationale and aims of democracy promotion as practiced by the West: Arab activists attacked the double standards practised by Western governments in the region and this made the existing strategies of gradual liberalization through working with autocratic governments obsolete. This is despite the fact that, as some have argued, gradual and measured promotion of democratic values in the political but especially civil society of autocratic states in the pre-2011 period actually contributed to the fertile ground for the revolts to happen (see, for example, Abrams 2011; 2012; Snider and Faris 2011).

There is little doubt that the Arab Spring constituted a wake-up call for democracy promoters, even though Western governments have welcomed, admittedly sometimes dragging their feet while so doing, the eastbound democratic march that started in Tunisia and Egypt. They have generally praised these developments. Nevertheless, these are testing times for democracy promotion. Having dealt only partially with the backlash against their activities in the wake of the debacle in Iraq and Afghanistan, where democracy remains elusive, democracy promoters are now facing their biggest challenge yet: how to support democratic transition in a region renowned for its diversity and volatility? The way democracy promoters will deal with this challenge will shape the contours of what democracy promotion will look like in the forthcoming years.

The critical approach we put forward here makes some important provocations and contributions to discussion about the future of democracy promotion. As we set out in the introduction, although the critical approach brings up many points of contention and criticism in democracy promotion, it is not necessarily a 'negative' approach. In this concluding chapter, reflecting on the critical study of democracy promotion conducted here, and the challenging global political context, we ask: how should democracy promoters deal with and think about democracy promotion today?

We do so in the context of the discussions in the previous chapters but with a specific focus on the challenges presented in the Middle East and North Africa today. The questions and issues we address in this book are, in one way or another, relevant to and magnified by the events of the Arab Spring. The sheer complexity of the situation exemplifies the need for democracy promotion to be revisited in order to address the main criticisms it faces: that democracy promotion is a neo-colonial venture that seeks to open economies to capitalist interests, that it imposes Western values, that it attempts to covertly implement regime change, and that it is merely an instrument of foreign policy; in brief that democracy promotion seeks to perpetuate the domination of the West over the rest.

We examine in this chapter the consequences of each of the critical questions we have raised in this book for our evaluation of democracy promotion in the Arab Middle East. We then seek to bring to bear our conclusions to this specific context. We will show that opportunities as well as challenges to revisit and rethink democracy promotion exist in the current context when we survey democracy promotion from a critical angle developed here.

Specifically, we argue that there is scope, in current democracy promotion, for better acknowledgement of the contextual and contested nature of democracy as a concept. We argue that while 'a liberal politico-economic model' has tended to dominate in democracy promotion since the 1990s, it would be a mistake to believe that making reference to a single model of thinking on democracy is adequate. Indeed, we argue that a complex pattern of democratic political development characterizes the Arab region's advances towards democracy. As Thomas Carothers recently reminded us, 'Middle East regimes are much more diverse than was the case in Central and Eastern Europe. The Arab world contains reformist monarchs, conservative monarchs, autocratic presidents, tribal states, failing states, oil-rich states, and water-poor states' (Carothers 2011). Future political life in the Middle East and North Africa will likely resemble Forrest Gump's box of chocolates: we are not sure of what we will get once it open's up; and democracy promoters need to be attuned to this. Indeed, democracy promotion may not today be systematically tied to *liberal* democracy promotion (see Hobson and Kurki 2012; Kurki 2013).

The critical approach, Arab Spring and democracy promotion

In this book we have tackled a number of difficult and challenging analytical questions faced by democracy promoters, and democracy promotion scholars, in their engagement with this evolving policy agenda. In Chapter 2 we discussed the power relations between the different donors in the globalizing industry of democracy promotion. In Chapter 3 we discussed the challenging task of trying to decipher whether democracy promotion is about interests or values, or a bit of both. We show that interests and values are today intricately intertwined in democracy promotion, while also showing that the critical theory approach seems to indicate that we need to be aware of the ways in which the very nature of the values passed on in democracy promotion – liberal values and liberal model of democracy – can be tied to particular interests, in the globalization of liberal economic and societal structures.

In Chapter 4 we tackled the question of democracy promotion and regime change and argued, somewhat controversially, that while there are different scales of intervention apparent in democracy promotion and support today, democracy promotion as an activity (even in its 'softest' expressions on a sliding scale of democratic interventionism) can be conceived, from the critical approach, as an attempt to affect the nature of the regime in other states. In Chapter 5 we demonstrated that the critical approach also indicates that, while some methods of context-sensitivity have been introduced in democracy promotion, many power structures and relations still exist within the supposedly neutral methods of 'civil society assistance' or aid conditionality. In Chapter 6, on the other hand, we examined how the political and the economic are interconnected. A politico-economic reading of democracy promotion reveals the significance of the expectation that democracy will not undermine free workings of a liberal economy. In Chapter 7 we argued that while power and hegemonic relations are present in democracy promotion, resistance and challenges to hegemony are also apparent today, and that in fact new forms and contours of hegemonic power relations seem to be emerging in democracy promotion.

But what do these conclusions of the critical approach to democracy promotion give us in concrete terms in thinking about the challenges of democratization and democracy promotion? And given the political, economic and social shockwaves caused by the Arab Spring, in what way could these events lead us to think differently about the challenges of democracy promotion in North Africa and the Middle East?

Firstly, it would seem that the critical approach directs us to read the potential for transformation in North Africa and the Middle East in new ways because, through this approach, we may obtain a better and more rounded view of the motivations for actions of external actors in the region. The Arab Spring, for many critics of democracy promotion, presented just another opportunity to lambast the Western states for their support to dictators in the Middle East: the EU and the US have been held to account, almost single-handedly, for the durable autocratic regimes in these states (see Carothers 2011; Hanau Santini and Hassan 2012).

Yes, the US and the EU were reluctant to challenge the status quo in the region and prior to the Arab Spring have more often than not supported autocratic regimes rather than any real moves towards democratization. The balance between values and interests has been such as to make it difficult for key donors – EU and US especially – to reconcile their values and interests in a productive way. In this regard the Arab Spring presents an important opportunity. It allows the US and the EU to align their long-term interest in stability and prosperity and access to market with the ideas of 'democracy' and 'freedom' as their key guiding values as foreign policy actors.

As we observed in Chapter 3, the relationship between values and interests is an inherently complex one and a perennially challenging factor in democracy promotion. What the Arab Spring does demonstrate is that shifts in alignment of values and interests are possible. It demonstrates that such openings can create conditions in which foreign policy actors can shift and realign how interests and values in relation to the region are perceived. Crucially, this does not mean that relations with North Africa and the Middle East are now all of a sudden guided by 'values' – to accept such a naïve view would be to misunderstand the motivations of key democracy promotion actors. However, neither does this realignment mean that democracy promotion in North Africa and the Middle East today is simply about fighting for national interests. Interests are certainly intricately involved in decisions to engage and in discussions about how to engage in democracy facilitation in the region today, but they are intermixed with new opportunities to promote the values of liberal democracy and liberal markets, which are central to these donors in terms of their identity as well as their interests. In a sense, the recent developments then allow the 'hegemonic' actors to 'heal' wounds in their self-identity and coherence of their foreign policy activity (The White House 2011).

But what about the claim, that some critics make, that democracy promotion – the intervention in Libya in support of rebel forces, for example, or the funding of civil society actors in Egypt – are forms of attempted 'regime change'? These are provocative challenges, partly because, from our perspective, there is quite a lot of pertinence to these types of criticism.

It is the case that 'what kinds of regimes emerge' matters for the US or the EU, or the IFIs for that matter. If a nationalist, Islamist or a socialist set of regimes emerge, not only are liberal interests of donor states under some threat but so are liberal values in their universal projection of values of individual freedom and free markets. If this is the case then there is nothing particularly surprising about the EU and US wanting to have some say in how democracy is shaped in these countries.

From our perspective democracy promotion is about regime change, even in non-military intervention cases; yet, this does not mean that democracy promotion is an essentially 'bad thing'. Regime change has a negative connotation, but at its core, it is a descriptive term which captures the sense in which other countries seek to affect regimes of others. These processes have always played a part in international politics, for rarely have the norms of sovereignty been so respected that no interest in the regimes of other states have been shown. Nor is it the case that sovereignty needs to be overwhelmingly respected. Power relations, and emancipatory potential, flow across and beyond the principle of 'sovereignty' today: interventions of various kinds then may not necessarily be 'wrong' simply because they aim at 'regime change'. Normative and moral judgments here are very complex indeed. However, at a minimum it is crucial for us to avoid lapsing into conceptual categories which hide the continuum of power relations (coercive to consensual) embedded in democracy promotion.

But what about the claim that today the West simply supports democracy in North Africa and the Middle East, and that no promotion of a particular model is taking place here? This is a mistaken and dangerous illusion often reproduced by practitioners in defence of their projects and programmes, and underlying assumptions. If indeed it is the case that democracy promotion is about regime change even when soft tools such as democracy assistance or civil society support is given, this means that we need to be attuned to the relations of power which emanate from these attempts to render democracy promotion 'contextually sensitive'. As we saw in Chapter 5 multiple constraints on NGOs and civil society actors actually flow from the funding mechanisms, project priorities and modes of engagements of actors on the ground. This also takes place in Egypt, and more generally in the Middle East today.

Indeed, it is interesting to note that the aim in Libya and Egypt and elsewhere has been to encourage liberal democratic systems and liberal democratic actors while, at the same time, support to and understanding of social democratic or Islamist actors have been far more difficult to conduct. There are dangers in engagement with these actors, certainly if their views on democracy do not align with the values (and interests) of the key donors.

Thus, we have a system of engagement here which, as it does elsewhere, often favours the kinds of actors donors 'recognize' as democratic – those that work with a classical liberal democratic view – while others seem anti-democratic. Contextual sensitivity does not seem to extend to thinking about the very different ideological, economic and sociological context within which democracy's meaning in the Middle East is created (Sadiki 2004). This is partly why there is the rise of a new class of NGOs in these states, connected to the donors and the international agenda, but also potentially co-opted in their understandings of what counts as modern economy and democracy. Students of democracy promotion need to be mindful to the relations of power which may emerge from 'grass roots' types of support for democracy: even the most benign and soft forms of democracy promotion have embedded within them specific understandings of democracy and economy, for democracy promotion can never be 'neutral', and is rarely fully grass roots-driven.

But what about the accusation that the actions of democracy promoters in the Middle East are not only political but also attempt to reform the economies of countries subjected to democracy promotion? This is a powerful accusation, for even during the autocratic years, heavy neoliberal restructuring was the aim of IFIs and other donors. Indeed, many would suggest that the revolution in Egypt, for example, was a response to the unequal economic development within the state caused by neoliberalization of the economy (see, for example, Tran 2011). In terms of politico-economic thinking, little seems to have changed in the minds of the democracy promoters. Yes, it is recognized that the stability of the state depends on socio-economic measures being taken seriously in providing the conditions of stable democracy. Yet, the solutions proposed to the region's economic woes are much the same as before: liberalization of the economy, opening up to foreign capital and greater integration into liberal trade structures. There is then a politico-economic backdrop to democratization, which is, while separate from 'political' support, intricately tied to it. If democratization was to undermine the agenda of creating open, free markets connected with international trading systems, problems would arise for the key democracy donors. In this regard Robinson's warnings resonate powerfully: democracy promotion seems to be linked to advancement of economic liberalism.

However, in contrast to Robinson – who argues that there is a global capitalist class which drives this policy agenda in order to advance its own interests – we have argued that we need to be careful about where power resides and how it functions in democracy promotion. It does not, we discuss in Chapter 7, reside with economic actors per se: it is not as if democracy promotion is a tool of Western capital per se. However, the consensus on what democracy is does seem to reproduce the notion that, while no specific models are prescribed, if the model chosen in a target country would contravene basic liberal rights of property ownership, liberty, electoral rights, and the workings of a liberal economy, then democratization would be 'problematic', and in fact might not count as 'democratization' at all. While this may be the case for the donors, of course, on the ground the type of democratization that is called for by populations often directly contradicts the conception of democracy of the donors (Bridoux 2013).

This presents a central dilemma in the Middle East today, for, arguably, processes of renegotiation of liberal democracy are taking place on the ground currently. The grounding values of a liberal hegemony are being challenged, resisted and negated in some instances in how actors are engaging with the idea of democracy. There is nothing 'self-evident' about the liberal democratic model being the most attractive for the left critics or Islamic activists, while all can, simultaneously, perceive some practical benefits in engaging in an electoral process. Underlying practical engagements with basic electoral systems, deep-seated criticisms of highly 'liberal' individualist values persist.

This has important consequences for democracy promotion. If certain aspects of liberal democracy are in fact contested by target populations, how should the hegemony of the liberal democratic model respond to reposition its values and interests? How is consensus to be created on politico-economic order when we do not live in the era of victorious liberal capitalism as we did in the 1990s? And crucially, how should democracy promoters respond in this context? What models of democracy and economy should be promoted and how?

Beyond liberal democracy

It may be the case that in today's context the West and its democracy promoters must be prepared to be more open and flexible, at least in the first instance, in their dialogue with other states. They cannot dictate, for example, to the Egyptians and Tunisians what their constitution should be like or which rights (political, personal, socio-economic) should be prioritized. The clashes of rights claims have to be weighed within these contexts and different meanings of democracy may result from the divergences of value priorities people bring to the table in discussing what democracy means in Egypt or Tunisia. This is the challenge of democratization: it entails the institutionalization of a deeply contested concept, with multiple potential meanings for different actors.

Let us be clear, it is not the case that Arabs do not 'do' Western democracy and human rights. But neither is it the case that they cannot and should not draw on and weigh the importance of their own traditions of thought on democracy and equality.

While liberal traditions of democracy are important and worth a consideration, they are not the only, nor are they unified, and nor are they the most valuable, traditions in thinking about what democracy means. To attach the idea of democracy to liberal rights and individualism, after all, in many ways goes against the very majoritarian impulse of the concept of 'people power'. Liberal democracy has proved one useful way of delimiting the absolute control of 'mobs' in modern states; yet at the same time in delimiting democracy to representation through electoral process, it also puts forward a rather limited and unambitious vision of democracy.

This lack of 'self-evidence' of liberal democracy and the need to discuss its virtues in relation to different value systems needs to be born in mind today by democracy promoters. They must have the courage of their own commitments today: they need to, while sticking to their own liberal principles and even in arguing for them, also remain flexible to various different interpretations of democracy that may arise and not exclude actors on these grounds. The negotiation over models of democracy in the Bolivian context (Wolff 2011; 2012) provides a striking example of what needs to happen in relation to Egypt: there is not necessarily just one model of democracy in Egypt, just as there isn't in Bolivia, as different political and ideological viewpoints engage in debate on what 'democratization' means. Democracy promoters must remain, as they have tentatively in the case of Bolivia, attuned to the complexities and flexibilities that these debates entail for their own actions. The key principle should indeed be, as Wolff argues in relation to Bolivia, 'not to do harm' in the first instance. Instead of the imposition of a liberal democratic model, and the potential negative consequences this may have, Wolff calls for democracy promotion to facilitate 'inclusive processes of dialogue, constructive conflict resolution and the like'. The end point is not a specific model of democracy but 'a peaceful and inclusive *process* of constructing a model appropriate for the specific country [receiving democracy assistance]' (Wolff 2012: 128).

There is another related challenge, however, that faces the 'conceptual systems' of Western democracy support: the necessity of having to face up to how the 'economic' is managed within the 'democratic' in democracy assistance and support. In recent years there has been some rekindling of the relationship between development and democracy assistance practices, and some moves have been made towards recognizing the significant overlap between the concerns about economic development and democracy (Carothers 2009b). Yet, little conceptual or theoretical rethinking has emerged from this rekindling. Indeed, it seems that capitalism and democracy still provide the two key principles without which democracy promotion could not function.

What this assumed interconnection misses out, however, is that the relationship between democracy and capitalism is not a necessary one but rather a contingent, and historically and theoretically contested, one. Other politico-economic models of democracy, too, exist and are being argued for by different political actors. In these models the economy-democracy relationship is conceived of very differently. While the liberal democratic model has at its heart the separation of the economic from the political, radical democratic, participatory democratic, or cosmopolitan democratic models do not conceive of the economic and the democratic as separable but rather reconstitute their relationships in new ways. The participatory democrats, for example, argue for democratic controls over the work place as a crucial condition of adequate societal democratization, while the cosmopolitan democrats call for democratization of global financial and economic controls, something conceived to remain, at present, outside the sphere of not only states but also of 'political' concerns of 'liberal' democrats. In social democracy, on the other hand, it is essential to maintain a 'dual track' democratic representation: representation in the political sphere of the parliament and representation in the setting of levels of socio-economic reward. Social democracy is not just liberalism with a few added extras: it is at its heart a rather more radical 'dual track' model of democracy where democratic controls are set for wage-earning levels and thus for levels of profit vis à vis over welfare. All these models can go in part with a 'minimal' model of liberal democracy but they are also at their core more than just 'liberalism+' models: they envisage a reconstitution of the economy-democracy relationship and make it central to 'democratization' of society and political structures (see Kurki 2013: 113–16).

Our claim is that we need to, in today's context, think seriously about these alternative politico-economic models of democracy – and others. This is because we need to be able to deal with the social and political 'downfall' which results from weak economies and growing social disparities that economic liberalization of these states may result in. While liberalization is not necessarily a bad thing at all for the overall growth of these states, at the same time democratization is a process where the balance of democracy and economy needs to be actively taken account of, especially in the context of a global economic crisis of the liberal model. A more socio-economically attuned and open approach to democracy promotion may be crucial in opening up more workable alternatives in these states. In other words, the commonly accepted model of liberal democracy that is lauded by the West needs to display some degree of conceptual flexibility to take into account non-Western local political and economic realities. Democratization from below is needed, yes, as much as its facilitation from the outside: this, we argue, takes far less action from the Western states than it takes thinking about – and openness and flexibility towards – various different models of democracy. Western states can, and should insist on core liberal values and make the case for their institutionalization. Yet, for democratization to succeed, they also need to remain open to definitions of democracy from the ground up: from contexts that bring up not only different cultural but, perhaps more crucially, different politico-economic interests and conditions. Then, and only then, will democracy truly live up to its expectations.

But what does such a move in conceptualizing democracy promotion mean for practices of democracy promotion?

The future of democracy promotion

We suggest three pathways to revising the role and practices of democracy promotion in today's world.

Firstly, we suggest a move away from apolitical, neutral and technical instruments and funding structures that dominate contemporary democracy promotion work. Indeed, what the Arab Spring embodies is an alternative conception of what democracy is, and an expectation that donors of democracy assistance will acknowledge such a reality. We believe that one way to reinvigorate democracy promotion is for practitioners to embrace the conceptual diversity and celebrate a variety of values that characterize democracy. Such an exercise would most probably widen the scope and deepen the intensity of democracy promotion work through an improved dialogue with new partners – going beyond liberal democracy – in democratizing countries. Undeniably, to open the door to a conceptual debate about democracy with recipients would also be received with sympathy as donors would acknowledge that their approach might not be free of limitations and problems. Being conscious of the value-based essence of democracy would also temper the tendency to treat democracy promotion as if it was a value-neutral apolitical technical agenda.

There is no doubt that it is indeed necessary to assess the effectiveness of democratization programmes in recipient countries in order to enhance future democracy assistance programming. Yet, we argue that the reporting and management methods should be adapted to the nature of democracy promotion as a policy agenda. Democracy promotion is not a science but an art. Democracy is a concept that is notoriously difficult to measure, and is actually more reliant on subjective assessments, interpretations and dynamic processes not readily quantifiable. Consequently, management and funding processes should recognize that the most valuable forms of democracy support might not be simply demonstrated through indicators or charts. It is not easy to quantify dialogue and engagement with recipients, but this can nevertheless be very significant and worthwhile. Overall, democracy support would benefit from a move in the direction of less 'measurement' and 'competition' and more explicit discussion on democratic expectations. Through such debate democracy promoters may be able to seize a greater range and number of opportunities to support democratic aspirations. Sustained dialogue about what democracy can and should mean would likely also ensure more positive responses from recipients and non-traditional actors, which may hold democratic ideas that fall outside the classical liberal approach.

Secondly, democracy promoters must think about and frame how their work on democracy affects state-market relationships in 'target states' and with what consequences, and such reflection needs to be systematically embedded in democracy promotion, which is currently focused far too much on the 'political', while ignoring how work in the 'political' realm inevitably also structures the economic. From a critical perspective, we observe that all models of democracy formulate assumptions about the relationship between state and markets. Hence, it can be argued that all variants of democracy are 'politico-economic models of democracy'. To acknowledge that democracy is always about the political and the economic is crucial to understand key issues affecting democracy promotion: the role of important economic actors, such as international financial organizations, in structuring democracy and democracy support; the different views of democracy's meaning held by different actors; why the financial crisis affects debates on democracy so deeply; and why the development-democracy nexus needs to be not only acknowledged but revised as a central part of democracy support. What is crucial here is for democracy promoters to expand this awareness of the politico-economic nature of democracy and diversify the different possible politico-economic models of democracy that can be promoted. In turn, this would impact relationships between state, market and other actors, and the types of development and democracy support that are engaged in. Doing so would assist in advancing a form of democracy support that would have more purchase, more pluralism, more sensitivity and more dialogical engagements between donors and recipients.

Thirdly, democracy promotion must be more sensitive to the way local context shapes what is possible. Democracy promoters recognize rhetorically the need to consider local contexts of democratization (see, for example, the role of 'local ownership' in democracy promotion discussed at length in Chapter 5). Yet, in practice there is a great deal more to be done to put this principle into practice. The issue today is not only encouraging 'demand', but 'seeing' the demand in a new way. There is a need to reflect on democracy's multiple meanings, and through this process identify the often unrecognized democratic demands in target countries – made by the homeless, by trade unionists, by religious groups, by peasant organizations and many other actors. It is not just political parties, NGOs and other professional civil society movements that should be engaged with. Better entry points may be developed when democratic aspirations are not so readily funnelled into specific classical liberal democratic expressions, but are considered as democratic and supported even when non-institutionalized, informal, voluntary, non-professionalized, anti-Western or non-liberal. Democracy promoters need to directly tackle their selection biases through reflecting on their own assumptions: it is not only people 'like us' that are democrats and it is not just 'democrats like us' that have legitimate democratic aspirations. Democracy support has to take seriously the wide range of ways democracy can be understood and practiced.

The challenges faced today by democracy promoters arise from decades of practices that led to the identification of democracy promotion by recipients as merely an instrument of foreign policy in the hands of great powers. Claims of genuine commitment to democratic progress made by democracy promoters are often sneered at and democracy promotion today sounds rather hollow to many. Too often, democracy promotion is seen as an instrument of domination rather than emancipation. It is actually quite revealing that, in the wake of the rise against Hosni Mubarak, the most progressive segments of the Egyptian political society refused to be associated with US or EU democracy assistance offers for support.

Fundamentally, if democracy promotion is to be relevant today, and we believe that it should, democracy promoters must offer qualitatively different types of responses. We have tried to show two things in this book. We have tried to destroy myths about democracy promotion that present it as a cynical and instrumental strategy in the hands of powerful actors that seek to subjugate the weak. Democracy promotion can be such a negative and domination-seeking activity.

Yet, democracy promotion is above all complex, multidimensional and contested. And this is because what is promoted, democracy, is itself a formidably contested and complex concept. There is nothing simple in promoting something like democracy. The trouble today is that donors want democracy promotion to be simple, manageable and assessable. Yet, even the most 'neutral' and 'technical' democracy promotion programmes implicitly carry specific political and economic ideals, value-assumptions, ideological notions and selection biases. Paying attention to the value-laden nature of democracy promotion and reflecting on democracy's multiple meanings is both possible and necessary. Doing so should be the concern primarily of the donors, not just the recipients. What kind of democracy is on offer? What is demanded and why? How can different kinds of democracy be supported? A strategy that begins from self-reflection on values and prioritizes dialogue will not only be ethically desirable in 'democratizing' democracy promotion – in making sure democratic debate on multiple potential democratic futures is ensured – but also in rendering democracy support more practically credible and responsive, and potentially also more effective.

Appendix

Online resources on democracy promotion

African Peer Review Mechanism

A self-assessment mechanism within the African Union context to ensure that member countries respect adherence to commonly agreed standards of good governance.

http://aprm-au.org/?q=thematic-area/democracy-good-political-governance

Carnegie Endowment for International Peace (Democracy and Human Rights)

Very influential think tank based in the US, founded in 1910. Its Democracy and Human Rights Department is spearheaded by Thomas Carothers, one of the most prolific and respected expert on democracy promotion.

www.carnegieendowment.org/programs/global/index.cfm?fa=proj&id=101

DEMO Finland

A cooperative organization of political parties active in democracy promotion established in Finland.

www.demofinland.org/index.php/en/

Democracy Digest

Blog on democracy promotion and related issues run by the National Endowment for Democracy (NED). Updated daily with stories about democracy from literally every corner of the world.

www.demdigest.net/blog/

EU – Human Rights and Democracy

Essential documents outlining the EU's willingness to include human rights and the promotion of democracy in all its external policies.

http://ec.europa.eu/europeaid/what/human-rights/index_en.htm

European Endowment for Democracy (EED)

A recently established European civil society funding mechanism functional from 2013. Modelled on the US-based NED, the Brussels-based EED is an independent organization that promotes freedom and democracy though support for pro-democratic civil society organizations, movements and individual activists acting in favour of a pluralistic multiparty system.

http://democracyendowment.eu/

European Network of Political Foundations (ENOP)

A network of European political foundations active in the support of democracy worldwide. It is envisioned as a 'cooperation structure, serving as a communication and dialogue instrument between European political foundations and the Institutions of the European Union as well as civil society actors in the fields of democracy promotion and development cooperation'.

www.european-network-of-political-foundations.eu/cms/

European Partnership for Democracy (EPD)

An independent European organization that brings together various NGOs and actors who wish to act in support of democracy outside of the European Union.

www.epd.eu/

European Political Foundations

A selection of European organizations that are active in democracy promotion, together with their political affiliation:

- Friedrich Ebert Foundation, Germany (Social Democrats) – www.fes.de/ or for Washington Office – www.fesdc.org/

- Konrad Adenauer Foundation, Germany (Christian Democrats) – www.kas.de/wf/en/

- Friedrich Naumann Foundation, Germany (Free Democrats) – www.en.freiheit.org/Aktuell/790c/index.html

- Hanns Seidel Foundation, Germany (the Bavaria-based Christian Social Union) – www.hss.de/english.html

- Heinrich Böll Foundation, Germany (The Greens) – www.boell.org/

- Centerpartiets Internationella Stiftelse, Sweden (Centre Party) – www.centerpartiet.se/Lokal/cis/

- Jarl Hjalmarson Foundation, Sweden (Swedish Moderate Party) – www.hjalmarsonfoundation.se/

- Olof Palme International Centre (Swedish Social Democratic Party) – www.palmecenter.se/

- Swedish International Liberal Centre (Liberal Party) – http://silc.se/

Freedom House

Freedom House is an independent watchdog dedicated to the expansion of freedom around the world. Freedom House publishes an annual report on the state of freedom in the world, assessing how open and democratic countries are.

www.freedomhouse.org/

FRIDE

FRIDE stands for Fundacion par alas Relationes Internacionales y el Dialogo Exterior, a Madrid-based think tank with a focus on EU foreign policy. Its mission 'is to inform policy and practice in order to ensure that the EU plays a more effective role in supporting multilateralism, democratic values, security and sustainable development'.

www.fride.org/

International IDEA

IDEA stands for International Institute for Democracy and International Assistance. IDEA is an intergovernmental organization that provides democracy builders with expert knowledge about democratization, offers support for policy development and analysis, and supports democratic reform.

www.idea.int/

Journal of Democracy

Academic journal specializing in democracy promotion and democratization, created, funded and run by the NED.

www.journalofdemocracy.org/

Middle East Partnership Initiative (MEPI)

MEPI is a programme based in the US Department of State. MEPI supports civil society groups, political activists, and business leaders in their efforts for political and economic reform, government transparency, and accountability projects in the Middle East.

http://mepi.state.gov/

Millennium Challenge Corporation (MCC)

An independent US foreign aid agency, MCC develops aid compacts that link good governance and economic growth.

www.mcc.gov/

National Endowment for Democracy (NED)

Funded by the US Congress, the NED is an NGO that groups four institutes (National Democratic Institute, International Republican Institute, The Solidarity Centre, and the Center for International Private Enterprise) dedicated to the growth and strengthening of democratic institutions around the world.

www.ned.org/

Network of Democracy Research Institute (NDRI)

Global network of think tanks that conduct research and analysis on democracy, democratization and related topics in comparative government and international affairs.

www.ned.org/research/network-of-democracy-research-institutes-ndri

Network of Democracy Research Institute (NDRI) – Digital Library

Searchable database of references about democracy promotion and related issues published by members of NDRI.

http://socialhost05.inmagic.com/Presto/content/AdvancedSearch.aspx?uc=TkRSS
VZpZXdlcnxORFJJVmlld2Vy&&ctID=NTNCMzhENkYtNzZFRS00NEE2LTg5
NjItOEJGQUEyNTcwNjUz&AspxAutoDetectCookieSupport=1

Organization for Security and Co-operation in Europe (OSCE)

The world's largest regional organization. The OSCE has developed an impressive record of electoral assistance, good governance and human rights programmes throughout the world.

www.osce.org/

The Netherlands Institute for Multi-Party Democracy (NIMD)

One of the best-known and active multi-party institutes. It is a 'democracy assistance organisation of political parties in the Netherlands for political parties in young democracies'.

www.nimd.org/

The Washington Quarterly

Influential journal published by the Center for Strategic and International Studies. Especially relevant today for its extensive coverage of the Arab Spring and its consequences.

http://csis.org/twq/

UN Democracy Fund (UNDEF)

New York-based international organization funded by 41 UN member states. Its mission is to spread democracy worldwide by supporting civil society organizations, promoting human rights and encouraging the participation of all groups in democratic processes.

www.un.org/democracyfund/

US Department of State (Bureau of Democracy, Human Rights and Labor)

Bureau in charge of the formulation of democracy promotion and human rights protection policies from the perspective of US diplomacy. Works mainly at bilateral governmental level.

www.state.gov/j/drl/

USAID (United States Agency for International Development)

The world's largest financial contributor to democracy promotion programmes.

- Democracy, Human Rights and Governance – www.usaid.gov/
  what-we-do/democracy-human-rights-and-governance

- Bureau for Democracy, Conflict and Humanitarian Assistance –
  www.usaid.gov/who-we-are/organization/bureaus/bureau-democracy-
  conflict-and-humanitarian-assistance

- Center of Excellence on Democracy, Human Rights and Governance –
  www.usaid.gov/who-we-are/organization/bureaus/bureau-democracy-
  conflict-and-humanitarian-assistance/center

Westminster Institute

UK-based think tank promoting freedom and individual dignity through funding independent research.

www.westminster-institute.org/

World Bank Institute on Governance

A centre for World Bank's thinking and assistance on governance reform, including links to projects.

http://wbi.worldbank.org/wbi/topic/governance

World Bank's Worldwide Governance Indicators

The World Bank's influential governance indicators and recent data on progress of governance reform in relation to these indicators.

http://info.worldbank.org/governance/wgi/index.aspx#home

Bibliography

Abrahamsen, R. (2000) *Disciplining Democracy: Development Discourse and Good Governance in Africa*. London: Zed Books.

Abrahamsen, R. (2004) 'The Power of Partnerships in Global Governance', *Third World Quarterly* 25(8): 1453–67.

Abrams, E. (2011) 'In the Streets of Cairo. Proof Bush Was Right', *Washington Post*, 30 January. Available at www.washingtonpost.com/wp-dyn/content/article/2011/01/28/AR2011012806833.html (accessed 1 July 2013).

Abrams, E. (2012) 'A Forward Strategy of Freedom', *Foreign Policy*, 23 (23 January). Available at www.foreignpolicy.com/articles/2012/01/23/a_forward_strategy_of_freedom (accessed 1 July 2013).

Allawi, A.A. (2007) *The Occupation of Iraq. Winning the War, Loosing the Peace*. New Haven, CT: Yale University Press.

Ayers, A. (2006) 'Demystifying Democratisation: the Global Constitution of (neo) liberal Polities in Africa', *Third World Quarterly*, 27(2): 321–33.

Bachrach, P. and Baratz, M. (1969) 'Two Faces of Power', in Roderick Bell, Daniel V. Edwards and Robert H. Wagner, (eds), *Political Power: a Reader in IR Theory and Research*. New York: The Free Press, pp. 95–9.

Barr, J. (2005) 'Statement by Ambassador Joyce A. Barr. Official Launch of the Namibian Democracy Support Centre', 22 November. Available at www.usaid.gov/na/pdfdocs/11-22-05AmbLaunchofNDSC-pressFINAL.pdf (accessed 2 May 2012).

Barsh, R.L. (1992) 'Democratization and Development', *Human Rights Quarterly*, 14: 120–34.

Bicchi, F. (2006) '"Our size fits all": normative power Europe and the Mediterranean', *Journal of European Public Policy* 13(2): 286–303.

Boot, M. (2004) 'Myths about Neoconservatism', in Irving Stelzer, (ed.), *Neoconservatism*, London: Atlantic Books, pp. 43–52.

Bridoux, J. (2011a) *American Foreign Policy and Postwar Reconstruction. Comparing Japan and Iraq*. Abingdon: Routledge.

Bridoux, J. (2011b) 'It's the Political, Stupid: National versus Transnational Perspectives on Democratisation in Iraq', *The International Journal of Human Rights*, 15(4): 552–71.

Bridoux, J. (2013) 'US Democracy Promotion and the Arab Spring: A Problem of Language of Democracy?' Paper presented at 'Democracy Promotion: Hegemony, Resistance and the Shifting Discourses of Democracy in International Relations', Senate House, London, 1 February.

Bridoux, J. and Kurki, M. (2012) 'Interview with Barbara Haig, Deputy to the President of the National Endowment for Democracy'. Washington, DC, 26 March.

Bueno de M.B., Merron, J.D., Siverson, R.M. and Smith, A. (1999) 'An Institutional Explanation of the Democratic Peace', *American Political Science Review,* 93: 791–812.

Burnell, P. (2000) 'Democracy Assistance: The State of the Discourse', in P. Burnell (ed.) *Democracy Assistance: International Co-operation for Democratization.* London: Frank Cass, pp. 3–33.

Burnell, P. (ed.) (2000) *Democracy Assistance: International Co-operation for Democratization.* London: Frank Cass.

Burnell, P. (2011) *Promoting Democracy Abroad: Policy and Performance.* New Brunswick, NJ: Transaction Publishers.

Bush, G.W. (2000) 'Party Platform: Foreign Policy – The Middle East and Persian Gulf, Republican National Convention 2000, Philadelphia, Pennsylvania', in Stanford Political Communication Lab, (ed.), *In their Own Words. Sourcebook for the 2000 Presidential Election*, Stanford, CA: Stanford University.

Bush, G.W. (2002) *State of the Union Address*, Washington, DC, 29 January. Available at www.whitehouse.gov/news/releases/2002/01/20020129-11.html (accessed 12 September 2012).

Caraley, D. (1999) *The New American Interventionism: Lessons from Success and Failures.* New York: Columbia University Press.

Carothers, T. (1999) *Aiding Democracy Abroad: the Learning Curve.* Washington, DC: Carnegie Endowment for International Peace.

Carothers, T. (2006) 'The Backlash against Democracy Promotion', *Foreign Affairs,* 85(2): 55–68.

Carothers, T. (2007a) *US Democracy Promotion During and After Bush.* Washington DC: Carnegie Endowment for International Peace. Available at www.carnegieendowment.org/files/democracy_promotion_after_bush_final.pdf (accessed 15 December 2010).

Carothers, T. (2007b) 'A Quarter Century of Promoting Democracy', *Journal of Democracy* 18(4): 112–15.

Carothers, T. (2008) *Does Democracy Promotion have a Future?* Carnegie Endowment for International Peace. Available at www.carnegieendowment.org/publications/index.cfm?fa=view&id=20247 (accessed 16 September 2012).

Carothers, T. (2009a) *Revitalizing Democracy Assistance.* Carnegie Endowment for International Peace. Available at www.carnegieendowment.org/files/revitalizing_democracy_assistance.pdf (accessed 16 September 2012).

Carothers, T. (2009b) 'Democracy Assistance: Political vs. Developmental', *Journal of Democracy* 20(1): 5–19.

Carothers, T. (2011) 'Think Again: Arab Democracy', *Foreign Policy*, 10 March. Available at www.foreignpolicy.com/articles/2011/03/10/think_again_arab_democracy?print=yes&hidecomments=yes&page=full (accessed 18 June 2013).

Carothers, T. (2012) *Democracy Policy under Obama. Revitalization or Retreat?* Washington, DC: Carnegie Endowment for International Peace.

Carothers, T. and Youngs, R. (2011) 'Looking for Help: Will Rising Democracies Become International Democracy Supporters?' *Carnegie Paper* (July).

Carr, E.H. (1939) *The Twenty Year Crisis 1919–1939: An Introduction to the Study of International Relations.* London and Basingstoke: Macmillan.

Chan, S. (1984) 'Mirror, Mirror on the Wall … Are the Freer Countries More Pacific?', *Journal of Conflict Resolution* 28(4): 617–48.

Chandler, D. (2007) 'Hollow Hegemony: Theorising the Shift from Interest-based to Value-based International Policy-making', *Millennium,* 35(3): 703–23.

Chatham House (2012) Proceedings of conference 'Democracy Promotion in the Context of Democratic Opportunities and Politico-economic Crises', Chatham House, London, 24 May.

Cheibub, J.A. and Vreeland, J.R. (2010) *Economic Development and Democratization*. Baltimore, MD: Johns Hopkins University Press.

Chemonics (2012a) *Democracy and Governance*. Available at www.chemonics.com/OurWork/OurPractices/DandG/Pages/default.aspx (accessed 11 June 2013).

Chemonics (2012b) *Our Mission and Values*. Available at www.chemonics.com/OurStory/OurMissionAndValues/Pages/default.aspx (accessed 19 June 2013).

Chemonics (2012c) *Our Approach*. Available at www.chemonics.com/OurStory/OurApproach/Pages/default.aspx (accessed 19 June 2013).

Chomsky, Noam and Herman, Edward S. (1979) *The Washington Connection and Third World Fascism: The Political Economy of Human Rights, vol I*. Boston, MA: South End Press.

Clark, I. (2011) *Hegemony in International Society*. Cambridge: Cambridge University Press.

Clinton, H. (2009) 'Remarks on the Human Rights Agenda for the 21st Century', Speech at Georgetown University, Washington, DC, USA, 14 December. Available at www.state.gov/secretary/rm/2009a/12/133544.htm (accessed 11 December 2012).

Clinton, H. (2010) 'Civil Society: Supporting Democracy in the 21st Century', Speech at the Community of Democracies, Warsaw, Poland, 3 July. Available at www.state.gov/secretary/rm/2010/07/143952.htm (accessed 11 December 2012).

Cook, B. and Kothari, U. (eds), (2001) *Participation: the New Tyranny*. London: Zed Books.

Cox, M., Ikenberry, J. and Takashi, I. (2000) *American Democracy Promotion: Impulses, Strategies, and Impacts*. Oxford and New York: Oxford University Press.

Cox, R.W. (1981) 'Social Forces, States and World Orders: Beyond International Relations Theory', *Millenium: Journal of International Studies,* 10(2): 126–55.

Cox, R.W. (1996) 'Gramsci, Hegemony, and International Relations: an Essay in Method', in Robert W. Cox, with Timothy Sinclair, *Approaches to World Order*. Cambridge: Cambridge University Press, pp. 124–43.

Coyne, C. (2008) *After War: The Political Economy of Exporting Democracy.* Stanford, CA: Stanford University Press.

CPA (2003b) *Order No 39, Foreign Investment*, 19 September. Available at www.iraq coalition.org/regulations/20031220_CPAORD_39_Foreign_Investment_.pdf (accessed 18 June 2013).

Crawford, G. (2008) 'EU Human Rights and Democracy Promotion in Central Asia: From Lofty Principles to Lowly Self-interests', *Perspectives on European Politics and Society,* 9(2): 172–91.

Crawford, G. and Abdulai, A. (2012) 'Liberal Democracy Promotion and Civil Society Strengthening in Ghana', in Christopher Hobson and Milja Kurki, (eds), *The Conceptual Politics of Democracy Promotion*. Abingdon: Routledge, pp. 131–50.

Dahl, R.A. (1969) 'The Concept of Power', in Roderick Bell, Daniel V. Edwards and Robert H. Wagner, (eds), *Political Power: a Reader in IR Theory and Research*. New York: The Free Press, pp. 79–92.

Dahl, R.A. (2000) *A Preface to Economic Democracy*. Berkeley, CA: University of California Press.

Diamond, L. (1999) *Developing Democracy: Toward Consolidation*. Baltimore, MD: Johns Hopkins University Press.

Diamond, L. (2008a) 'Democracy in Retreat'. *Real Clear Politics*. Available at www.real clearpolitics.com/articles/2008/03/democracy_in_retreat.html (accessed 16 September 2012).

Diamond, L. (2008b) 'How to Save Democracy?' *Newsweek*, 31 December. Available at www.newsweek.com/2008/12/30/how-to-save-democracy.html (accessed 16 September 2012).

Diamond, L. (2008c) 'The Democratic Rollback: The Resurgence of Predatory State', *Foreign Affairs,* 87(2): 36–48.

Diamond, L. (2009) 'Supporting Democracy: Refashioning US Global Strategy', in Alexander T. J. Lennon, (ed.), *Democracy in US Security Strategy: From Promotion to Support*. Washington, DC: Center for International and Strategic Studies, pp. 29–54.

Dodge, T. (2010) 'The Ideological Roots of Failure: The Application of Kinetic Liberalism to Iraq', *International Affairs,* 86(6): 1269–86.

Dunia Frontier Consultants (2009) *Private Foreign Investment in Iraq. Update: November 2009*. Washington, DC, November. Available at http://iier.org/i/files/docs/Summary_of_Dunia_Private_Foreign_Investment_in_Iraq_Nov_2009.pdf (accessed 28 June 2010).

EED (2013) *Our Mission*. Available at http://democracyendowment.eu/ (accessed 19 June 2013).

Elliot, K.A. (1992) 'Economic Sanctions', in Paul J. Schraeder, (ed.), *Intervention into the 1990s. US Foreign Policy in the Third World*. Boulder, CO: Lynne Rienner, pp. 97–112.

Eurofound (2013) *Acquis Communautaire*. Available at www.eurofound.europa.eu/areas/industrialrelations/dictionary/definitions/acquiscommunautaire.htm (accessed 11 November 2013).

European Commission (2008) *Budget Support. The Effective Way to Finance Development?* Brussels: European Commission.

Forsythe, D.P. (1992) 'Democracy, War, and Covert Action', *Journal of Peace Research,* 29(4): 385–95.

Foucault, M. (2008) *The Birth of Biopolitics. Lectures at the College the France, 1978–1979*, Michel Senellart and Graham Burchell (eds). Basingstoke: Palgrave Macmillan.

Freedom House (2013) *Freedom in the World 2013. Democratic Breakthrough in the Balance*. Available at www.freedomhouse.org/sites/default/files/FIW%202013%20Booklet%20-%20for%20Web_1.pdf (accessed 6 June 2013).

Freyburg, T., Grimm, S. and Leininger, J. (2012) 'Do all Good Things Go Together? Conflicting Objectives in Democracy Promotion', *Democratization,* Special Issue, 19(3). Available at http://hdl.handle.net/1814/23960 (accessed 11 June 2013).

FRIDE (2010a) *Assessing Democracy Assistance*. Available at www.fride.org/project/19/assessing-democracy-assistance (accessed 19 June 2013).

FRIDE (2010b) *Friedrich Ebert Foundation*. Available at www.fride.org/publication/845/democracy-assistance,-the-facts:-friedrich-ebert-foundation-%28fes%29 (accessed 19 June 2013).

FRIDE (2012) *Democracy Assistance Factsheet. Sweden*. Available at www.fride.org/publication/868/democracy-assistance,-the-facts:-sweden (accessed 11 June 2013).

Fukuyama, F. (1989) 'The End of History and the Last Man', *The National Interest* (Summer). Available at www.kropfpolisci.com/exceptionalism.fukuyama.pdf (accessed 14 June 2013).

Gallie, W.B. (1956) 'Essentially Contested Concepts', *Proceedings of the Aristotelian Society*, 56: 167–98.

GAO (2005) *Rebuilding Iraq. US Water and Sanitation Efforts Need Improved Measures for Assessing Impact and Sustained Resources for Maintaining Facilities*. Washington, DC: United States General Accountability Office, September. Available at www.gao.gov/new.items/d05872.pdf (accessed 18 June 2013).

GAO (2007a) *Stabilizing and Rebuilding Iraq. Conditions in Iraq Are Conducive to Fraud, Waste, and Abuse*. Washington, DC: United States General Accountability Office, April. Available at www.gao.gov/new.items/d07525t.pdf (accessed 18 June 2013).

GAO (2007b) *Rebuilding Iraq. Reconstruction Progress Hindered by Contracting, Security, and Capacity Challenges*, Washington, DC: United States Government Accountability Office, February. Available at www.gao.gov/new.items/d07426t.pdf (accessed 18 June 2013).

GAO (2008) *Stabilizing and Rebuilding Iraq. Actions Needed to Address Inadequate Accountability over US Efforts and Investments*. Washington, DC: United States General Accountability Office, March. Available at www.gao.gov/new.items/d08568t.pdf (accessed 18 June 2013).

Gebel, A. (2012) 'Dealing with Dislocations: International Anticorruption Discourse and Neoliberal Hegemony'. Paper presented at International Studies Association Annual Convention, San Diego, USA, 1–4 April.

Gebel, A. (2013) 'The Ideal within: Conceptions of Politics, Economics and Civil Society in the International Anticorruption Discourse', PhD thesis, Aberystwyth University.

George, A. (1991) *Western State Terrorism*. Cambridge: Polity Press.

Gill, S. (1986) 'Hegemony, Consensus and Trilateralism', *Review of International Studies*, 12(3): 205–21.

Gills, B. and Rocamora, J. (1992) 'Low Intensity Democracy', *Third World Quarterly*, 13(3): 501–23.

Gills, B., Rocamora, J. and Wilson, R. (1993) *Low Intensity Democracy: Political Power in the New World Order*. London: Pluto Press.

Gramsci, A. (1971 [1929–35]) *Selections from the Prison's Notebooks*, edited and translated by Q. Hoare and G. Novell Smith. London: Lawrence and Wishart.

Gwertzman, B. (2011) 'Egypt: a "Textbook" Foreign Policy Dilemma', Interview with James A. Baker III, *Council on Foreign Relations*, 2 February. Available at www.cfr.org/africa/egypt-textbook-foreign-policy-dilemma/p23984 (accessed 11 June 2013).

Hanau S., Oz, R and Oz, H. (2012) 'Transatlantic Democracy Promotion and the Arab Spring', *The International Spectator*, 47(3): 65–82.

Harvey, D. (2003) *The New Imperialism*. Oxford: Oxford University Press.

Harvey, D. (2007) 'Neoliberalism as Creative Destruction', *The Annals of the American Academy of Political and Social Science*, 610: 21–44.

Hearn, J. (2000) 'Aiding Democracy? Donors and Civil Society in Africa', *Third World Quarterly*, 21(5): 815–30.

Held, D. (1996) *Models of Democracy*. 2nd edn. Oxford: Polity.

Hermann, M.G. and Kegley Jr, C.W. (1998) 'The US Use of Military Intervention to Promote Democracy: Evaluating the Record', *International Interactions*, 24(2): 91–114.

Herring, E. and Rangwala, G. (2006) *Iraq in Fragments. The Occupation and Its Legacy*. London: Hurst and Company.

Hindess, B. (1996) *Discourses of Power. From Hobbes to Foucault*. Oxford: Blackwell

Hobson, C. and Kurki, M. (eds) (2012) *The Conceptual Politics of Democracy Promotion*. Abingdon: Routledge.

Hollis, M. and Smith, S. (1990) *Explaining and Understanding International Relations*. Oxford: Clarendon Press.

Huntington, S. (1991) *The Third Wave: Democratization in the Late Twentieth Century*. Norman, OK: University of Oklahoma Press.

Hyde-Price, A. (2008) 'A "Tragic" Actor"? A Realist Perspective on "Ethical Power Europe"', *International Affairs* (Royal Institute of International Affairs) 84(1): 29–44.

Ikenberry, G. Knock, T.J., Slaughter, A.-M. and Smith, T. (2009) *The Crisis of American Foreign Policy: Wilsonianism in the Twenty-first Century*. Princeton, NJ: Princeton University Press.

Ish-Shalom, P. (2006) 'Theory as a Hermeneutical Mechanism: The Democratic-peace Thesis and the Politics of Democratization', *European Journal of International Relations,* 12(4): 565–98.

Jackson, P.T. (2011) *The Conduct of Inquiry in International Relations*. Abingdon: Routledge.

Joes, A.J. (ed.) (1999) *Saving Democracies: US Intervention in Threatened Democratic States*. Westport, CT: Praeger Publishers.

Joseph, J. (2012) *The Social in the Global.* Cambridge: Cambridge University Press.

Juhasz, A. (2006) *The Bush Agenda. Invading the World, One Economy at a Time*. London: Duckworth.

Kagan, R. and Kristol, W. (1996) 'Toward a Neo-Reaganite Foreign Policy', *Foreign Affairs,* 75(4): 18–32.

Kagan, R. and Kristol, W. (eds) (2000) *Present Dangers. Crisis and Opportunity in American Foreign and Defense Policy*. San Francisco, CA: Encounter Books.

Kagan, R. and Kristol, W. (2004) 'National Interest and Global Responsibility', in Irving Stelzer, (ed.), *Neoconservatism*. London: Atlantic Books, pp. 55–74.

Kegley Jr., Hermann, C.W. and Margaret G. (1997) 'Putting Military Intervention into the Democratic Peace: A Research Note', *Comparative Political Studies,* 30(1): 1–21.

Kerr, J. (2009) 'The Biggest Problem we Face is Keeping our Independence. Party Oppression of Civil Society in the "New" Iraq'. Available at www.lse.ac.uk/Depts/global/ Publications/DiscussionPapers/DP45.doc (accessed 13 December 2012).

Kiely, R. (2005) *Empire in the Age of Globalisation. US Hegemony and Neoliberal Disorder*. London: Pluto Press.

Kissinger, H. (1994) *Diplomacy*. New York: Simon and Schuster.

Korosteleva, E.A. (2011) 'Change or Continuity Is the Eastern Partnership an Adequate Tool for the European Neighbourhood?', *International Relations,* 25(2): 243–62.

Krasner, S.D. (2011) 'Foreign Aid: Competing Paradigms', *Journal of Intervention and Statebuilding,* 5(2): 123–49.

Krauthammer, C. (2004a) 'Democratic Realism. An American Foreign Policy for a Unipolar World'. Speech given at the 2004 Irving Kristol Lecture, AEI Annual Dinner, 10 February. Available at http://gees.org/documentos/Documen-053.pdf (accessed 9 July 2013).

Krauthammer, C. (2004b) 'In Defense of Democratic Realism', *The National Interest.* Available at http://web.clas.ufl.edu/users/zselden/Course%20Readings/Krauthammer.pdf (accessed 9 July 2013).

Kurki, M. (2010) 'Democracy and Conceptual Contestability: Reconsidering Conceptions of Democracy in Democracy Promotion', *International Studies Review,* 12(3): 362–86.

Kurki, M. (2011) 'Governmentality and EU Democracy Promotion: The European Instrument for Democracy and Human Rights and the Construction of Democratic Civil Societies', *International Political Sociology,* 5(4): 349–66.

Kurki, M. (2013) *Democratic Futures: Revisioning Democracy Promotion*. Abingdon: Routledge.

Laclau, E. and Mouffe, C. (2001) *Hegemony and Socialist Strategy: Towards a Radical Democratic Politics.* London: Verso.

LaFeber, W. (1965) *John Quincy Adams and American Continental Empire*. Chicago, IL: Quadrangle Books.

Lake, D.A. (1992) 'Powerful Pacifists: Democratic States and War', *American Political Science Review,* 86: 24–37.

Lawson, S. (1993) 'Conceptual Issues in the Comparative Study of Regime Change and Democratization', *Comparative Politics,* 25(2): 183–205.

Layne, C. (1994) 'Kant or Cant: The Myth of the Democratic Peace', *International Security,* 19(2): 5–49.

Lennon, A.T.J. (2009) *Democracy in US Security Strategy: From Promotion to Support.* Washington, DC: Center for International and Strategic Studies.

Lipset, S.M. (1959) 'Some Social Requisites of Democracy: Economic Development and Political Legitimacy', *The American Political Science Review,* 53(1): 69–105.

Litwak, R.S. (2007) *Regime Change: US Strategy through the Prism of 9/11.* Washington, DC: Woodrow Wilson Center Press.

Lukes, S. (1974) *Power. A Radical View.* Basingstoke: Palgrave Macmillan.

Lukes, S. (2005) *Power. A Radical View,* 2nd edn. Basingstoke: Palgrave Macmillan.

Lynch, G. and Crawford, G. (2011) 'Democratization in Africa 1990–2010: an Assessment', *Democratization,* 18(2): 275–310.

McClintock, M. (1992) *Instruments of Statecraft.* New York: Pantheon Books

McFaul, M. (2004–05) 'Democracy Promotion as a World Value', *Washington Quarterly,* 28(1): 147–63.

McFaul, M. (2010) *Advancing Democracy Abroad: Why we Should and How we Can.* Lanham, MD: Rowman and Littlefield.

Mandelbaum, M. (2007) *Democracy's Good Name: The Rise and Risks of the World's Most Popular Form of Government.* New York: Public Affairs.

Mansfield, E.D. and Snyder, J. (1995) 'Democratization and War', *Foreign Affairs,* 74(3): 79–97.

Mansfield, E.D. and Snyder, J. (2005) *Electing to Fight: Why Emerging Democracies Go to War.* Cambridge, MA: MIT Press.

Maoz, Z. and Abdolali, N. (1989) 'Regime Types and International Conflict', *Journal of Conflict Resolution,* 33(1): 3–35.

Maoz, Z. and Russett, B. (1993), 'Normative and Structural Causes of Democratic Peace 1946–1986', *American Political Science Review* 87(3): 624–38.

Martinot, S. (2003) 'The Cultural Roots of Interventionism in the US', *Social Justice,* 30(1): 113–31.

MCC (2007) *MCC and the Long Term Goal of Deepening Democracy.* Washington, DC: MCC. Available at www.mcc.gov/documents/reports/mcc-112007-paper-democracy.pdf (accessed 4 May 2012).

MCC (2011) *Report on the Criteria and Methodology for Determining the Eligibility of Candidate Countries for Millenium Challenge Account Assistance for Fiscal Year 2011.* Washington, DC: MCC. Available at www.mcc.gov/documents/reports/report-2010001039502-selection-criteria-and-methodology.pdf (accessed 13 June 2013).

MCC (2013) *Programs and Activities.* Available at www.mcc.gov/pages/activities (accessed 10 November 2013).

Meernik, J. (1996) 'United States Military Intervention and the Promotion of Democracy', *Journal of Peace Research,* 33(4): 391–402.

MNF-I (2007) 'Iraqi First Program Surpasses $ 1 billion for Year'. Available at www.usf-iraq.com/?option=com_content&task=view&id=12881&Itemid=128 (accessed 18 June 2013).

Muravchik, J. (1991) *Exporting Democracy. Fulfilling America's Destiny.* Washington, DC: American Enterprise Institute Press.

NED (undated) *Statement of Principles and Objectives*. Washington, DC: NED. Available at www.ned.org/publications/statement-of-priniciples-and-objectives (accessed 20 October 2010).

NED (2007) *Strategy Document*. Washington, DC: NED. Available at www.ned.org/docs/strategy/strategy2007.pdf 9 (accessed 20 October 2010).

NED (2012) *2012 Strategy Document*. Washington, DC: NED. Available at www.ned.org/docs/strategy/2012StrategyDocument.pdf (accessed 12 June 2013).

Nicholson, M. (1996) 'The Continued Significance of Positivism?' in Steve Smith, Ken Booth and Marysia Zalewski, (eds), *International Theory: Positivism and Beyond*. Cambridge: Cambridge University Press, pp. 128–45.

Orbie, J. (2009) *Europe's Global Role*. Farnham: Ashgate Publishing.

Paris, R. (2010) 'Saving Liberal Peacebuilding', *Review of International Studies,* 36(2): 337–66.

Peceny, M. (1999) *Democracy at the Point of Bayonets*. University Park, PA: Pennsylvania State University Press.

Petrova, T. (2011) 'From Recipients to Donors: Why Young Democracies Become Democracy Promoters', *APSA 2011 Annual Meeting Paper*. Available at http://ssrn.com/abstract=1899971 (accessed 11 June 2013).

Pickering, J. and Peceny, M. (2006) 'Forging Democracy at Gunpoint', *International Studies Quarterly,* 50(3): 539–60.

Plattner, M.F. (1993) 'The Democratic Moment', in Larry Diamond and Marc F. Plattner, (eds), *The Global Resurgence of Democracy*. London: John Hopkins University Press, pp. 26–38.

Potter, D. (1997) 'Explaining Democratization', in David Potter, David Goldblatt, Margaret Kiloh and Paul Lewis, (eds), *Democratization*. Cambridge: Polity Press, pp. 1–37.

Prestowitz, C.V. (2003) *Rogue Nation: American Unilateralism and the Failure of Good Intentions*. New York: Basic Books.

Przeworski, A. (2000) *Democratization and Development: Political Institutions and Well-being in the World, 1950–1990*. Cambridge: Cambridge University Press.

Pridham, G. (2005) *Designing Democracy: EU Enlargement and Regime Change in Post-Communist Europe*. Basingstoke: Palgrave Macmillan.

Reagan, R. (2004) 'Address to members of the British Parliament, June 8, 1982', in *Speaking My Mind: Selected Speeches*. New York: Simon and Schuster.

Reisman, W.M. (2004) 'The Manley O. Hudson Lecture: Why Regime Change is (Almost Always) a Bad Idea', *The American Journal of International Law,* 98(3): 516–25.

Robinson, W.I. (1996) *Promoting Polyarchy*. Cambridge: Cambridge University Press.

Robinson, W.I. (2004) 'What to Expect from US "Democracy Promotion" in Iraq', *New Political Science,* 26(3): 441–7.

Russett, B. (1990) *Controlling the Sword*. Cambridge, MA: Harvard University Press.

Sadiki, L. (2004) *The Search for Arab Democracy: Discourses and Counter-Discourses*. London: Hurst & Company.

Schimmelfennig, F. and Scholtz, H. (2008) 'EU Democracy Promotion in the European Neighbourhood: Political Conditionality, Economic Development and Transnational Exchange', *European Union Politics,* 9(2): 187–215.

Schmitter, P.C. and Karl, T.L. (1993) 'What Democracy Is ... and Is Not', in Larry Diamond and Mark F. Plattner, (eds), *The Global Resurgence of Democracy*. Baltimore, MD: Johns Hopkins, pp. 49–62.

Schumpeter, J. (1947) *Capitalism, Socialism and Democracy,* 2nd edn. London: Allen and Unwin.

Schweller, R. (2000) 'US Democracy Promotion: Realist Reflections', in Michael Cox, G. John Ikenberry and Takashi Inoguchi, (eds), *American Democracy Promotion: Impulses, Strategies, and Impacts*. Oxford: Oxford University Press, pp. 41–62.

Sen, A. (1999) 'Democracy as a Universal Value', *Journal of Democracy,* 10(3): 3–17.

Shadid, A. (2010) 'Thousands Protest Electricity Shortage in Iraq', *The New York Times*, 19 June. Available at www.nytimes.com/2010/06/20/world/middleeast/20iraq.html (accessed 18 June 2013).

Shah, R. (2011) '2011 Annual Letter'. Available at http://50.usaid.gov/wp-content/uploads/2011/03/USAID-Annual-Letter-Digital-04-06-11.pdf (accessed 28 May 2011).

Showstack A.A, (ed.) (1982) *Approaches to Gramsci*. London: Writers and Readers.

Smith, S., Booth, K. and Zalewski, M. (1996) *International Theory: Positivism and Beyond*. Cambridge: Cambridge University Press.

Smith, T. (2007) *A Pact with the Devil. Washington's Bid for Supremacy and the Betrayal of the American Promise*. New York: Routledge.

Smith, T. (2012) *America's Mission: The United States and the Worldwide Struggle for Democracy*, 2nd edn. Princeton, NJ. Princeton University Press.

Snider, E.A. and Faris, D.M. (2011) 'The Arab Spring: US Democracy Promotion in Egypt', *Middle East Policy*, 18(3): 49–62.

Sullivan, M.J. (2008) *American Adventurism Abroad: Invasions, Interventions, and Regime Changes since World War II*. Oxford: Blackwell Publishing.

Teivainen, T. (2009) 'The Pedagogy of Global Development: the Promotion of Electoral Democracy and the Latin Americanisation of Europe', *Third World Quarterly,* 30(1): 163–79.

The White House (2011) 'Remarks by the President on the Middle East and North Africa' (19 May). Available at www.whitehouse.gov/the-press-office/2011/05/19/remarks-president-middle-east-and-north-africa (accessed 19 June 2013).

Tran, M. (2011) 'Arab Activists Criticise Conditions Attached to Western Aid', *The Guardian*, 27 June. Available at www.guardian.co.uk/global-development/2011/jun/27/arab-activists-criticise-western-aid (accessed 9 July 2013).

Tyler, P. E. (1991) 'After the War. Bush Links End of Trading Ban to Hussein Exit', *The New York Times*, 21 May. Available at www.nytimes.com/1991/05/21/world/after-the-war-bush-links-end-of-trading-ban-to-hussein-exit.html (accessed 1 June 2012).

UNESCO (2002) *The Interaction between Democracy and Development*. Paris: Unesco. Available at www.unesco.org/new/en/social-and-human-sciences/themes/democracy/report-on-democracy-and-development/ (accessed 27 June 2013).

UNSC (1990) *Resolution 661*, 6 August. Available at: http://daccess-dds-ny.un.org/doc/RESOLUTION/GEN/NR0/575/11/IMG/NR057511.pdf?OpenElement (accessed 31 May 2012).

UNSC (1991a) *Resolution 687*, 3 April. Available at: http://daccess-dds-ny.un.org/doc/RESOLUTION/GEN/NR0/596/23/IMG/NR059623.pdf?OpenElement (accessed 31 May 2012).

UNSC (1991b) *Resolution 688*, 5 April. Available at: http://daccess-dds-ny.un.org/doc/RESOLUTION/GEN/NR0/596/24/IMG/NR059624.pdf?OpenElement (accessed 31 May 2012).

USAID (2012) 'Interview with Joe Taggart, USAID Democracy Officer. "Inclusive, Transparent, and Credible": A Witness to Tunisia's Historic Elections', *Frontline* (January/February). Washington, DC: USAID.

US Department of State (2011) *DRL: Democracy*. Available at www.state.gov/j/drl/democ/ (accessed 25 September 2013).

Vincent, J. (1987) 'Freedom and International Conflict: Another Look', *International Studies Quarterly,* 31(1): 103–12.

Weede, E. (1984) 'Democracy and War Involvement', *Journal of Conflict Resolution,* 28(4): 649–64.

Whitehead, L. (1996) *The International Dimensions of Democratization: Europe and the Americas.* Oxford: Oxford University Press.

Whitehead, L. (2002) *Democratization: Theory and Experience.* Oxford: Oxford University Press.

Whitehead, L. (2009) 'Losing "the Force"? The "Dark Side" of Democratization after Iraq', *Democratization,* 16(2): 215–42.

Wilson, W. (1917) *War Messages,* 65th Cong., 1st Sess., 2 April. Available at http://wwi.lib. byu.edu/index.php/Wilson's_War_Message_to_Congress (accessed 11 June 2013).

Wolff, J. (2011) 'Challenges to Democracy Promotion: the Case of Bolivia'. Carnegie Paper. Available at http://carnegieendowment.org/files/democracy_bolivia.pdf (accessed 19 June 2013).

Wolff, J. (2012) 'The Conceptual Politics of Democracy Promotion in Bolivia', in Christopher Hobson and Milja Kurki, (eds), *The Conceptual Politics of Democracy Promotion.* Abingdon: Routledge, pp. 119–30.

Youngs, R. (2001) *The European Union and the Promotion of Democracy: Europe's Mediterranean and Asian Policies.* Oxford: Oxford University Press.

Youngs, R. (2003) 'European Approaches to Democracy Assistance: Learning the Right Lessons?' *Third World Quarterly,* 24(1): 127–38.

Youngs, R. (2008) *Is the European Union Supporting Democracy in Its Neighbourhood?* Madrid: FRIDE. Available at www.fride.org/download/librofride.pdf (accessed 7 June 2013).

Youngs, R. (2010) *The European Union and Democracy Promotion: a Critical Global Assessment.* Baltimore, MD: John Hopkins University Press.

Youngs, R. (2012) 'Misunderstanding the Maladies of Liberal Democracy Promotion', in Christopher Hobson and Milja Kurki, (eds), *The Conceptual Politics of Democracy Promotion.* Abingdon: Routledge, pp. 100–16.

Zogby, J. (2012) 'Should America Be Involved in Democracy Promotion in the Arab World?', *The Huffington Post,* 14 April. Online. Available at www.huffingtonpost. com/james-zogby/us-arab-relations_b_1425554.html (accessed 17 April 2013).

Index